New Frontiers in Healthcare Management

Nonfiction Books by Deborah Shlian, MD, MBA:

Women in Medicine and Management (editor) American College of Physician Executives, 1995

Clinical Concepts in Medical Practice Management (contributor) McGraw-Hill, 1996

MD/MBA: Physicians on the New Frontier of Medical Management (contributor) American College of Physician Executives, 1998

In Search of Physician Leadership (contributor) Health Administration Press, 1998

New Frontiers in Healthcare Management

MBAs Evolving in the Business of Healthcare

Deborah Shlian, MD, MBA
and
Clint Patterson, PhD, MBA

Writers Club Press
San Jose   New York   Lincoln   Shanghai

New Frontiers in Healthcare Management
MBAs Evolving in the Business of Healthcare

All Rights Reserved © 2001 by Deborah Shlian, MD, MBA

No part of this book may be reproduced or transmitted in any form or by any means, graphic, electronic, or mechanical, including photocopying, recording, taping, or by any information storage retrieval system, without the permission in writing from the publisher.

Writers Club Press
an imprint of iUniverse.com, Inc.

For information address:
iUniverse.com, Inc.
5220 S 16th, Ste. 200
Lincoln, NE 68512
www.iuniverse.com

ISBN: 0-595-17435-3

Printed in the United States of America

Contents

The Healthcare Management Marketplace:
Opportunities and Challenges 1

The Value of an MBA 13

Managed Care Administrator 21

Managed Care Physician 29

Managed Care Physician Executive 37

Integrated Delivery System Executive 47

Insurance Company Executive 61

Associate Hospital Chief of Staff 69

Consultant 75

Entrepreneur 82

Information Systems Executive 87

Medical Director: Resources and Outcomes 98

Management Search Firm CEO 110

Physician Executive in Training 121

Where We Have Come From and Where We are Headed 129

Unpredictable Paths–Not for the Faint Hearted 135

A Lifelong Relationship 143
Final Words 147
About the Editors 151
Additional Resources 153

LIST OF ILLUSTRATIONS

MBAs conferred 15

LIST OF TABLES

Table 1: Median HMO salaries 12

Foreword

This monograph sets out to document the career paths that fifteen individual healthcare managers have taken. These are people who have found success in many different areas within the healthcare management field. They include the roles of medical director, hospital administrator, insurance company executive, information systems manager, consultant, financial officer and entrepreneur. All of these contributors have graduated from UCLA's Anderson School of Management with MBA degrees and part of each story is how the degree has helped or hindered their opportunities. Their stories are compelling. Readers embarking on a healthcare management career, or even those already on a career path, may learn from their failures as well as successes that each has found along the way.

List of Contributors

Deborah Shlian, MD, MBA
Clint Patterson, PhD, MBA
Robin Mackenworth, MBA
Joe Spooner, MD, MBA
Charles Payton, MD, MBA
Eleanor Brewer, MEd, MBA
Alan Bramson, MBA
David Auerbach, MD, MBA
Greg Vigen, MBA, FSA
Richard Eidinger, MD, MBA
Mike Wall, MBA
Gail Grant, MD, MPH, MBA
Dave Snell, MD, MBA
Mark Strom, MD, MBA
Susan Acevedo, MD, MBA

THE HEALTHCARE MANAGEMENT MARKETPLACE: OPPORTUNITIES AND CHALLENGES

Deborah Shlian, MD, MBA

Writing about the healthcare marketplace is akin to trying to hit a moving target. The unprecedented size and pace of change within the past three decades has produced an enormous transformation in the delivery of America's healthcare. A new set of rules is being written—a new marketplace dynamic emerging. This latest paradigm is being built on ever-higher standards of cost effectiveness and quality. Success is benchmarked against economic as well as clinical criteria as never before. And within this chaotic landscape, the leadership challenges facing today's healthcare organizations have never been greater. As we enter the new millennium, the general consensus among industry analysts is that the purchaser, provider and customer relationships will evolve into something completely different from that of the past. To the extent that one can look at trends to predict the future, there are a number listed below that for the near future will likely create more and new opportunities at all levels for healthcare managers as organizational and role restructuring continues.

Managed Care Enrollment Still on the Rise

Although the penetration of managed care clearly differs by geographical regions, there is little doubt that managed care will continue to be a dominant theme in the near future. The overall unbridled growth of HMOs (up from 58 million in 1995 to more than 170 million plus members in the year 2000), has not only affected commercial products, but Medicare and Medicaid beneficiaries as well. Nationally, HMO enrollment is flat, while PPO enrollment is on the rise. The Washington-based Alliance for Health Care Reform reports that health insurance premiums, which had been holding steady since 1992, began to rise well above the general rate of inflation.[1] According to the same source, in 1999, employer-based health plans raised premiums by an average of 7.3%—nearly three times the general inflation rate. For benefit year 2000, consultants at Mercer project health insurance costs to climb 7.5% to about $4500 per worker with this trend expected to continue for several years to come. At the same time, the Alliance reports that the double-digit rates of managed care growth seen in recent years will slow. The consensus is that health plans will have to come up with innovative ways to squeeze additional savings out of the system if spending growth is to remain moderate. As new members move into HMOs, their special needs are creating opportunities in such areas as home health which for Medicare recipients is paid for by Medicare part A. According to the Wall Street Journal, in the 1990's home health spending soared 30% a year with $16 billion spent in 1995.[2]

On the physician side, the managed care trend has virtually turned many physician practices inside out–especially in more mature markets. Most managed care organizations' reliance on primary care and the current

---

[1] Alliance for Healthcare Reform. 2000. How We Got It Anyway, The Clinton Health Plan Never Died. *Managed Care*, 9 (10): 22-28.
[2] Anders, G. 1997 Home Healthcare, *Wall Street Journal*, March 6.

emphasis on the gatekeeper model has reversed the preferred ratio of primary care physicians to specialists. At the same time, other companies like United Health have advanced alternatives through a so-called "open access" model. Blue Shield in California adopted a limited Access Plus program, although overall the company still relies on delegated (traditional) contracting. Carve-outs have developed in such areas as oncology, cardiology and mental health–allowing specialists direct access to patients with high cost acute and/or chronic illness. All these kinds of changes in managed care create an increased need for information and information systems for the development, monitoring and measuring of disease management outcomes, physician profiles, and medical case management initiatives.

Integration and Consolidation of the Marketplace: More Mergers and Alliances?

The "bigger is better" business environment of the 1990's spurred a rush of mergers among HMOs and other managed care companies, particularly in markets that were vertically integrated or those with an excess of specialists and hospital beds. Mergers also occurred among and between hospitals, insurers and physician groups. Large academic medical centers merged with healthcare delivery systems (e.g. Cornell and Mount Sinai). Physician groups formed alliances with hospitals, becoming ever larger, super PHOs (e.g. BJC Health System with 16 hospitals and over 2500 physicians; Unity Health System with 11 hospitals and over 1300 physicians). Local HMOs merged with one another or are being acquired by large insurers (e.g. PCA by Humana, CareFlorida by Foundation Health).

Paradoxically, dozens of new HMOs sprang up in 1996 at the same time that existing HMOs consolidated. The total number of HMOs jumped from about 550 in 1993 to about 630 in 1996 according to InterStudy, including about 60 new HMOs formed in 1995 alone. Many of the new HMOs were local, physician owned plans. Provider run plans were especially popular in states such as Georgia as newly passed insurance regulation became favorable to their formation. Of the dozen or so HMOs that applied for licenses in Georgia in 1995, about half were physician owned.

As data on the fate of these organizations is collected, it appears that across the country HMOs lost a collective $187 million during 1999 despite the positive performance of most of the country's largest, publicly traded managed care organizations (with over 500,000 members).[3] Chairman Martin Weiss, of Weiss Ratings, stated that the disparity between smaller and larger plans is growing. The 34 largest HMOs posted aggregate profits of $753 million. Of the smaller plans, 57 percent of those with fewer than 100,000 members lost money. To the extent that HMOs pursue economies of scale and market clout through mergers and acquisitions, small HMOs may continue to be targets for larger companies, although since early 1999 this trend has been at a standstill in specific regions such as California. Some predict that many physician owned plans will not be able to survive against large, well capitalized insurers while others feel that local, provider owned plans will band together to become favorable opponents to regional and national insurers.

Regardless of who is ultimately correct, one trend seems clear: health professionals are beginning to take a much more active role in managed care. In fact, some analysts have called this phenomenon the rise of the physician executive. According to an industry consultant, all groups of physicians who have succeeded in the long term both qualitatively and operationally have involved physician led, physician driven change. "Regimes that are externally

---

[3] Marcille, J.A. 2000. "Large HMOs Do Well While Small Ones Slide." *Managed Care*, 9 (10): 14.

imposed and most often anchored in purely economic assumptions will not bear the fullest fruit and could even backfire."[4]

If real, this could affect future management career opportunities for both physician and non-physician executives since the market for managers in general may be weakening. A 1996 article in the National Business Employment Weekly cited a new phenomenon of layoffs of the most senior level managers, creating a glut of candidates in a consolidated market. Since that time, this trend has only accelerated. It is not surprising then that administrators might resent physicians honing in on their territory. To compete for scarce positions paying annual base salaries of $150,000 and up, managers must have impressive leadership and marketing skills. The non-physician administrators are often individuals who have spent 10 to 20 years making very low salaries relative to physicians (see Table 1), moving up through the ranks from areas like underwriting, contracting, sales and marketing.[5] For physician managers, the catch-22 is that many who seek senior level opportunities are not afforded the same kind of exposure as their non-physician counterparts to these key areas.

RISING PRESCRIPTION COSTS

As the US Presidential elections loomed in 2000, the issue of prescription costs took center stage. In 1999 Americans spent well over $100 billion on prescription drug costs or about 10 cents of every dollar spent on healthcare.[6] That trend is expected to accelerate: while healthcare expenditures in

---

[4] Gerber, P.C., Bojlefeld, M. 1997. "What's Ahead for Managed Care in 1997: The Shape of Medical Care Hangs in the Balance." *Physician's Management,* January: 36-47.

[5] Solomon, G. 1997. "Demand Weakens for HMO Executives, *National Business Employment Weekly."* September 22-36.

[6] Day, K. 2000. "The Driving Force: What's really behind runaway health care costs?" *The Washington Post,* January 9.

general are increasing at a rate of 7-10 percent, drug expenditures are rising 17-20 percent.

Intense Pressure on Employers to Continue to Provide Health care Benefits to Employees

When negotiating new contracts with employer groups in the mid to late 1990s, insurers were forced to maintain low premium prices as employers and consumers refused to tolerate huge boosts. However, market forces fueled principally by higher prescription drug costs, an aging population and higher costs of medical technology have finally prevailed and premiums are on the rise again. Many large employers have thrown in the towel on the ability of HMOs to manage costs and have begun to consider shifting away from the defined benefit approach toward defined contributions. According to healthcare consultant and author, Peter Boland, PhD, defined contribution could "radically change the interaction and the accountability among employers, employees/patients, providers and health plans. I see at least seven distribution sources that could take over the distribution function now performed by health plans. You have insurance companies, niche channel players, Internet portals, clearing houses, health benefit outsourcers, established retailers and system integrators."[7] With defined contribution, an individual employee could still choose a traditional managed care option such as HMO or PPO, but would have more ownership of the money spent on his own healthcare. At the same time that insurers are having a more difficult time negotiating advantageous contract terms, hospitals and physician groups are regaining bargaining clout by becoming more savvy negotiators. Again, this trend has opened doors for those physician executives with

---

[7] Marcille, J.A. 2000. "Predicting MCOs' Future by Learning from the Past: A Conversation with Peter Boland, PhD." *Managed Care*. 9 (9): 37-45.

contract negotiation skills to participate in an area heretofore off limits to them as at least some insurers understand the value of someone who can speak to the providers in their language and at the same time appreciate the business issues. At the same time, non-physician managers with hard business and financial expertise are able to command higher salaries for their skills.

Increased Consumer Voice

Continuing a trend first noted in 1996, consumers are becoming more vocal and assertive about the quality of their medical care. As managed care became the norm in many markets around the country, consumers pushed for quality safeguards, flexibility to seek care outside the network and full disclosure of plan restrictions. While some see legislative solutions like mandatory 48-hour hospitalization following childbirth a fad, consumers have spoken and healthcare organizations that want to stay in business are heeding the message that the managed care industry is going to be under close scrutiny. In California, there are at least thirty new healthcare laws that took effect in 2000-2001 including the Mental Health Parity provision. This is compounded by the fact that many employer groups are considering increasing employee contributions to their health benefits. As the public is given more responsibility for their healthcare purchasing decisions, there is more incentive to understand what they are buying. This trend has produced a growing number of quality measures or at least proxies for quality such as NCQA's HEDIS and patient satisfaction surveys. Healthcare executives with interests and training in epidemiology, health policy research and preventive medicine (generally with MPH degrees) increasingly found new job opportunities with insurers, provider groups, consulting firms, employer groups and research institutions as a result of this trend.

One of the trends that has emerged as a result of consumer demand for access to healthcare information has been the rise in health web sites. And just as quickly as they were established, many of these sites foundered as easy access to venture capital dried up in early 2000. Despite their financial woes, industry analysts and professionals expect at least the big-name companies to survive by merging with other institutions1. Several e-health ventures, such as Drkoop.com and HealthGate Data Corp., have seen their stock value plummet in the wake of low revenue intake. Jeffrey Peters, a financial analyst at Dain Rauscher Wessels in Minneapolis, said most of the early consumer health care sites all sought advertising revenue, but "there was not enough advertising money to support the sites that sprang up." The web sites that have survived are the larger entities that have "paired with other institutions, such as employers, insurers, hospitals or clinics, that will pay to supply information to customers."

Three companies that fit this model are WebMD, Medem.com, and Intelihealth. WebMD has acquired 10 companies in 2000 in its effort to specialize in health care transactions online. Medem.com provides information supplied by the American Medical Association and other medical groups. Intelihealth is a subsidiary of Aetna U.S. Healthcare, the country's largest operator of HMOs. Intelihealth has built a diverse revenue stream" through advertising and the sale of health-related products from its web site. It also has a partnership with Harvard Medical School and the University of Pennsylvania School of Dental Medicine. Intelihealth will also introduce a new service in 2001 year that will give subscribers their own health web site and e-mail information bulletins. David Kramer, CEO of Medical Broadcasting Co., a medical marketing firm, feels that such consolidation is a bad harbinger for less established and smaller health care web sites. "If we're lucky, there will be 50 web sites left standing, and they will be the big brands. The smaller, harder to find ones will be the ones that disappear." He added, "Now we are just in this early part of the information end that makes it difficult for people to make money purveying information alone. People who are willing to pay for it, like the pharmaceutical companies, will have to create more fundamental partnerships."[8]

Next Stage Cost Reductions

Up until 2000, while there was significant progress in cost reduction, much of it was low hanging fruit such as reducing hospital stays. The next stage is going to involve much more substantive changes in healthcare delivery, particularly for the sickest five percent of the population for whom we spend an estimated 60 percent of all medical care dollars. Integrated health information systems, aggressive, internet-based disease management programs, outcomes measurement are all seen as strategies to reduce costs and thus opportunities for medical managers—again particularly for those with specialized technical skills and training.

HEALTH INSURANCE PORTABILITY AND ACCOUNTABILITY ACT OF 1999 (HIPAA)

The Health Insurance Portability and Accountability Act of 1999 (HIPAA) which protects health insurance coverage for workers and their families when they change or lose their jobs is expected to have a huge impact on the health care system. Publication of the final rules will establish national formats and data content standards for electronic claims and related transactions, create technical and administrative procedures to ensure the security of electronic health data, and forge policies to protect the confidentiality of medical information. In addition to the administrative and operational ramifications, HIPAA will also have a significant financial impact on health care. Many industry observers expect provider and payer organizations to spend more money on HIPAA compliance than they did to make their information systems 2000 compliant. As an example, at least two Blue Cross Blue Shield plans—Highmark, Inc in Pittsburgh, Pennsylvania and Horizon Blue Cross Blue Shield in Newark, New Jersey—predict that their HIPAA budgets will match their Y2K budgets.[9]

HIPAA will require health care organizations to establish formal, stringent procedures on how health information is handled internally and by business partners. It requires the retraining of all employees that handle identifiable information in new procedures governing the use and disclosure of information. It requires physical safeguards to protect computer systems and information technology to control and monitor access to data and secure data in transit. The proposed security and privacy rules also require health care organizations to conduct risk assessments to determine where they are vulnerable to security or privacy lapses, ascertain the degree of acceptable risk, and implement appropriate administrative and technical policies. Organizations must document and justify the risk assessment; federal officials can at any time audit an organization's HIPAA compliance.

In addition, the Joint Commission on Accreditation of Health Care Organizations (the Oak Brook Terrace, Ill.-based firm that accredits hospitals) is considering making HIPAA compliance a part of its accreditation requirements.

---

[9] Goedert, J. 1999 "The Dawn of HIPAA." *Health Data Management*. April: 84

Ultimately, HIPAA will require a fundamental change in how provider and payer organizations conduct business. Clinicians, administrative staff, researchers and others will be forced to change their day-to-day routine. "This is not just an information technology issue-it is an operational issue that will reach out and touch every area of a health care organization," says Thomas Hanks, practice director for HIPAA compliance at Beacon Partners Inc., a Hoffman Estates, Ill.-based health care consulting firm.

Bottom Line

The bottom line is that the rate of change sweeping America's healthcare delivery system continues to accelerate. In this new environment, leadership roles for healthcare executives are much more varied and often more focused in specific "specialty areas" (such as Quality Management, Medical Informatics, Disease Management) than even a few years ago. While opportunities abound, there is often far less job security within many organizations today than ever before. Given these issues, how should you as a medical manager deal with this uncertainty? First: acknowledge it. Second: decide if you want to be a part of it. If you do, study emerging trends and target opportunities compatible with your skills, training and interests. Finally: go for it!

Table 1: Median HMO Salaries[10]

By Plan Enrollment

Position	All Plans	<25K	25-50K	50-100K	100-200K	200K+
CEO	187,038	150,000	153,687	187,038	214.860	260,000
Assoc.CEO	131,000	99,007	125,048	119,461	152,934	218,000
General Manager	110,000	90,000	83,160	112,000	115,986	175,000
General Counsel	95,000	90,000	52,000	71,000	92,566	105,000
CFO	109,990	90,000	100,000	100,268	112,392	148,900
Finance Director	70,721	60,000	51,750	61,000	75,364	81,533
Operations Director	80,000	69,084	68,000	75,500	85,000	85,000
Operations Manager	54,000	51,100	45,000	58,840	55,010	63,000
Controller	65,002	58,127	59,380	63,500	72,508	85,000
Chief Accountant	50,000	45,000	45,000	47,760	52,000	59,688
Purchasing Manager	43,460	33,109	35,000	41,322	46,000	54,600
VP Planning/Dev	111,682	115,000	100,000	113,332	105,000	139,100
Dir. Planning/Dev	75,000	63,524	61,950	77,500	75,000	79,023
Underwriting Mgr	60,860	61,500	52,000	57,498	60,755	66,235
VP Human Res	100,000	91,000	95,720	90,092	92,000	118,000
Dir Human Res	65,000	50,617	52,000	63,954	71,255	75,000
Personnel Mgr	49,200	43,113	40,000	45,150	54,000	54,500
Comp.Benefits Mgr	54,148	45,000	40,000	56,000	49,100	64,891
Dir. Quality Assur.	57,000	53,000	55,000	50,857	60,000	63,346
Dir. Utiliz. Review	58,000	55,000	53,1	58,023	61,766	62,550
Dir. Case Mgmt	61,916	58,850	55,770	57,648	65,000	64,475
VP MIS	120,000	102,120	90,000	114,000	106,728	140,000
Dir. MIS	72,116	59,307	62,138	68,400	80,000	87,480
Systems/Prog. Mgr	57,071	50,000	50,620	57,555	57,246	66,800
Operations Mgr	52,140	46,896	46,109	47,019	56,000	59,376
VP Claims Admin	91,609	80,017	85,000	89,658	93,000	112,500
Dir Claims Admin	67,299	60,650	53,000	55,000	69,004	75,790
Claims Mgr	45,000	41,600	42,924	41,385	47,000	51,713
Chief Marketing Off	112,000	95,472	90,753	101,500	114,650	136,655
Marketing Dir	70,000	56,277	63,000	76,778	75,000	75,554
Sales Mgr	56,883	57,642	48,575	57,331	55,750	57,946
Member Svc Mgr	43,323	40,000	42,000	42,700	45,000	47,483
Chief Med Off	190,000	190,000	185,000	160,000	170,636	204,750
Medical Director	155,000	150,000	150,000	150,298	157,186	161,761
Asst. Med. Dir	135,000	130,000	126,866	129,996	132,300	138,477
Dir. Provider Rels	65,200	61,416	62,500	67,000	63,378	78,019
Dir. Network Dev	69,330	66,483	63,300	66,200	73,992	58,262
Mgr. Network Dev	55,882	55,000	50,003	53,980	60,000	56,000

10 *"The HMO Salary Survey"* Spring, 1996. Rockford, IL: Warren Surveys

THE VALUE OF AN MBA

Clint Patterson, PhD, MBA

Your true value depends entirely on what you are being compared with.
                                                                Bob Wells

What is the value of a Masters in Business Administration (MBA) for the healthcare professional? That question isn't easily answered because value is situation specific. If the measure of value for a degree is the extent to which it helps the holder to successfully, even creatively, perform his or her work, then the MBA has value–but only in combination with the individual's own qualities, skills, and characteristics, and in the right work context.

Throughout this book the reader will find many examples where the degree, education and training offered at the Anderson School of Management (a.k.a. AGSM for those who graduated more than a couple of years ago!) has been personally and professionally invaluable to the writer. This chapter has a different purpose. It looks at several facets of the "value" of an MBA, so that healthcare professionals thinking about obtaining an MBA or current MBAs thinking about applying their talents in healthcare will have a more rounded perspective on the value of the degree.

Before the value of an MBA can be addressed, it is important to try to clarify just what an MBA is. While this might seem obvious at first, picking up an application, course catalog or annual report from Anderson or almost any other leading business school will quickly reveal that today there are many different kinds of MBAs. In obtaining the degree, it is possible to select a major concentration in a variety of disciplines, obtain certificates in a number of special areas (including healthcare) or even combine the degree with a concurrent JD, MD, MN, or MPH, just to name a few. As a result, it becomes difficult to describe the properties or characteristics of an MBA. (Defining other degrees would prove equally challenging.) I will therefore have to make observations about something that doesn't actually exist: a "generic" MBA. Given that limitation, then we ask, to whom and in what context does the MBA have value?

Value to the Degree Holder

For the degree holder, a legitimate question is the extent to which an MBA can be helpful in obtaining a good professional situation in healthcare. Here the ubiquitous business school concepts of supply and demand can provide some interesting benchmarks to assess the value of an MBA.

Supply:

Graduate education in business has grown tremendously over the years. In 1971, only 25,977 MBAs were awarded; since 1980, the number of Master's degrees conferred in business has risen an average of four percent per year. According to the American Academy of Colleges and Schools of Business, 187,655 students were enrolled in graduate business programs as of Fall, 1995, an increase of almost 11.5 percent from the Fall of 1993 (168, 307). Only one Master's degree is more popular than the MBA, and that is the Master's in education, but that difference is shrinking (98,938 MEd's in 1997 versus 93,437 MBAs).

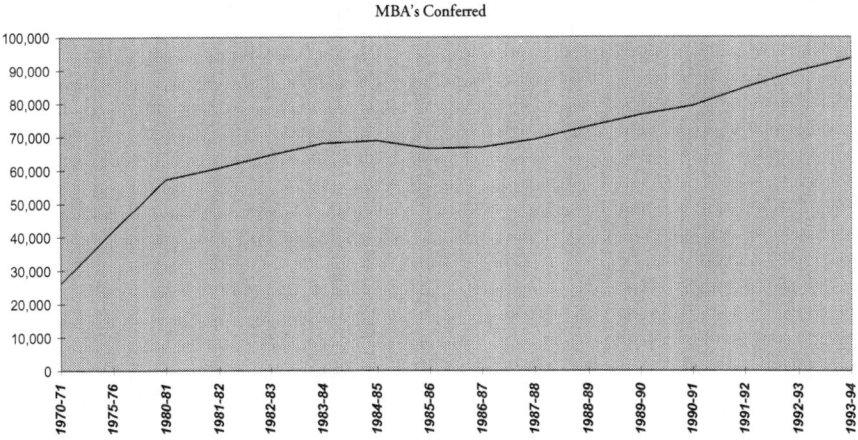

Source: U.S. Department of Education, National Center for Education Statistics

Demand:

With respect to measuring demand for MBAs graduating from their training programs, the challenge is a little bit tougher, although it should not be dramatically different from supply in the long run. One indirect measure of demand is the number of newly minted MBAs from top schools who are employed three months after graduation. According to a survey by U.S. News and World Report, the median proportion of employed new graduates from its ranking of the top 25 ranked schools was 98 percent. Obviously this is an extremely limited index and it does not address graduates from non-ranked schools or those who undertake their own entrepreneurial ventures (See Wall Street Journal, Managing Your Career, page B1, June 13, 1997, for some insight into entrepreneurial MBAs at Anderson). Moreover, this figure focuses only on those with fresh degrees and ignores the demand for experienced MBAs.

Similar problems exist if one attempts to use the average starting salaries for new graduates as a proxy for demand. US News & World Report also ranks business schools by starting salaries (the range for 1995 average was from a high of $73,500 for Stanford graduates, down to $50,000 for those from University of Maryland at College Park; Anderson graduates earned an average of $63,000).

However, it can also be argued that money is a relatively poor proxy for measuring value, demand or other characteristics, particularly in fields that are not entirely driven by the profit motive (such as healthcare or education). In these fields, salaries may simply be low, and graduates choosing to enter those fields must accept that reality–which does not say that the degree lacked value in helping them achieve satisfying employment in their chosen field.

What can be said with certainty is that incoming students must perceive potential value in the degree, because they are voting with their feet. Demand for admissions to the Anderson School is strong. In one recent year, the school had received 3870 applications for the 300 expected positions in its MBA Class of 1999–roughly one position for every 13 applicants.

Value to the Employer

For the employer, the MBA offers proof of certain intellectual qualities or capabilities–those required to get the degree. In this sense, it is the school that adds value to the degree holder, and that process begins even before he or she sets foot on campus. In assessing candidates, the Anderson School Admissions Committee uses a comprehensive set of criteria for allocating the slots in each year's class. The GMAT serves as one piece in the puzzle. The median GMAT scores for the class of 1998 was 650. Applicants are also carefully evaluated in terms of undergraduate

GPA, additional educational training and work experience. In addition, "leadership ability," extracurricular accomplishments and other personal characteristics play a role in the admissions process. The school's admission screening process ultimately complements prospective employer's selection processes by serving as a first pass review. In effect, it pre-screens candidates for positions in management and highlights potential targets for hiring.

Of course the primary value added by the school is through the didactic course work (in every subject from accounting to theory Z). Students will be exposed to the "core" curriculum, graduating with an understanding of accounting, finance, information systems, strategy, human resources and statistics. In addition, informal training in teamwork, presentation skills, analytic thinking, and a wealth of other experiences contribute immensely to the value of the degree. An MBA represents a tremendous amount of work and variety of experience, which many organizations value highly.

Still, for the employer, the MBA degree will be worthless if the candidate is not a good fit with the firm or company and with the position. As Deborah Shlian points out in her chapter, it takes a great deal of research and careful consideration to make that determination. The recruitment and selection process is a fine but imperfect science. Any selection or classification system is going to be limited and the MBA degree is only one consideration among a variety of factors. An employer has to look beyond the degree *per se* to the actual requirements of the position and the full range of qualities and capabilities that the candidate can offer. There will always be excellent managers, consultants and administrators who chose not to or never had the opportunity to go through business school. Similarly, there will be poor ones who march right in with the finest grades and credentials—right down to their MBA from a top school. The person is not the degree, and the degree is not the thing of value.

As a psychologist, I have come to see the MBA as a "diagnostic" marker–a beginning point. For example, there is a good chance that someone with an MBA in finance will be an excellent resource in analyzing a merger or acquisition. At the same time, other characteristics, such as a lack of appreciation for the humanistic elements of an organization may render that person unhelpful or even destructive to the project at hand. As one of my favorite clinical supervisors once phrased it "they were a great [professional] before they went to that school…or maybe in spite of that school, but not because they got a degree from that school!" In the real world, an individual's value is demonstrated in their approach to listening, questioning, analyzing and answering tough questions. The degree *per se* means nothing in terms of day to day activities. At the same time, it is often the ticket one needs to "play the game" or work in healthcare management.

The Value of an MBA in Healthcare: A Personal Perspective

In my first management position, I tackled problems with a common sense approach but no formal training. While this sufficed much of the time, I must admit that I was often unaware of additional factors and considerations that might have rendered a different or more effective approach. Through the lectures, seminars, readings and case analyses at Anderson I was able to benefit from the knowledge and experience of professors, guest speakers and my classmates. They helped me to see alternative interventions and approaches to management and the delivery of healthcare services that would have a positive impact for patients and staff alike. I came to realize that formal management and administrative training offers to healthcare organization is embodied in the focus, discipline, and exposure to organizational principles that the Master's program provides.

Looking back on an earlier stage of my career, one of the things that perplexed me was the apparent gap between the administrators and clinicians present in large organizations. There always seemed to be a certain level of mistrust and miscommunication between these two groups. The clinicians complained that policies and programs were arbitrary, ill conceived and would not have a positive impact on patient care. For their part, it seemed that administrators perceived the clinicians as prima donnas forever whining about every little change that was introduced–people who could not understand the competitive nature of the business and should only deal with patients.

Many of us who are active in the field of healthcare have found that the value of a clinical degree can be greatly enhanced by an MBA and vice versa. As our healthcare delivery system grows more complex and competitive, there is a greater need for people who can understand the situation from the patient's side AND the administrative side. My hope is that the Anderson school will continue to attract healthcare professionals and lay persons interested in applying management techniques in the field of healthcare.

Leveraging the clinical with the administrative skills has turned out to be a personally rewarding and exciting strategy for me. The number of healthcare professionals, including physicians applying to and completing MBA programs is growing rapidly. The Anderson school has recently introduced a combined MD/MBA program (along with the established MPH/MBA program). There were seven students with healthcare backgrounds in the Fully Employed MBA Class of 1999, and seven physicians in the Executive MBA Class of 1999, and the number of applicants with healthcare backgrounds seeking these degrees from Anderson is increasing every year. Other schools such as UC Irvine and Wharton have specialized tracks or certificate programs within their management programs. Such programs are gaining in popularity and reflect the tremendous demand for skilled, formally trained managers in the healthcare arena.

In Closing:

The value of an MBA for healthcare professionals transcends purely economic considerations. Obviously there are many employers, including some in healthcare, who favor graduates from MBA programs. Many are willing to pay a premium for such credentials. Against this measure of value, it is worth recalling the words of Albert Einstein:

> *One should guard against preaching to young people success in the customary form as the main aim in life. The most important motive for work in school and in life is pleasure in work, pleasure in its result, and the knowledge of the value of the result to the community.*

It is also important to reiterate that the person is not the degree and the degree is not the thing of value. Consider the "value" of an MBA in its broadest context. For the employer and the degree holder, its value is situational–that is, it must be held by a person with the right additional qualities and characteristics, in the right company and the right situation. It has no absolute value–only a value for the individual given the task at hand.

Managed Care Administrator

Robin Mackenroth, MBA

Past Career

I felt the earliest inklings of a medical career while attending Stanford University. I considered going "pre-med", but decided against it when I looked at all the "weed out" courses that were required. Instead, I ventured into a health care administration career when I decided to major in human biology. The course work in human biology definitely helped prepare me for my future career, because I learned not only about the scientific side of medicine (e.g., biochemistry, physiology, genetics, etc.), but also about the business of medicine (e.g., accounting, statistics, economics, decision making, etc.). The challenging Stanford curriculum had side benefits; it taught me that I could persevere against incredible odds (e.g., tight deadlines) and fueled my desire for continuous learning.

My first "real" job upon graduating from Stanford was with the Management Engineering Department at Desert Hospital in Palm Springs, California. The studies that I worked on there allowed me to learn about hospital operations from the ground up. I spent several hours in the Laboratory for a space planning project, and even more hours in the Emergency Room trying to figure out what the "psychotic" head nurse's staff was doing. I developed a technical focus early on in my career, and knowing basic analytical techniques has subsequently served me well.

Despite the euphoria of living and working in Palm Springs, I soon learned why people jokingly referred to my employer as "Desperate" Hospital. The hospital had lost several million dollars before I joined the staff in late 1987, but I naively assumed that they would not lay me off after paying to move me to Palm Springs only seven months before. I was wrong. Luckily, however, my employer had a heart, gave me two months to find a job, and sent me to expensive outplacement counseling. I learned an important skill: networking with members of my profession. I definitely put that new skill into practice, since my boss had given me free use of the phones to find a new job (a mistake he came to regret). I called everybody I knew in professional societies I belonged to and requested additional names from each person I talked to. After a month of frenzied calling, I got an interview with Kaiser Permanente in Pasadena, California. Ironically, my current boss referred me to my future boss and a job that I would not necessarily have been aware of if I were not networking like crazy.

I spent the next four years in the Management Engineering Department at Kaiser Permanente. I started as an Analyst, and because of my good technical skills, I was able to complete my work accurately and quickly. However, I learned that technical skills would only advance my career so far. The softer, "people" skills became increasingly important to my opportunity for promotion. I hated to deal with company "politics", but I learned quickly that that was unavoidable. My introduction to "politics" occurred at the lunch table. I had made some comments to my peers about some frustrations I was having with a big project, and my comments were interpreted such that my boss thought I was refusing to do my job. The truth eventually came out, but I learned an important lesson: I needed to be careful about what I said and how I said it, even to those I thought I could trust. Controlling my emotions continues to be a challenge, as I am an outgoing person who prefers to vent rather than get an ulcer. However, I have learned to pick my battles more wisely.

Despite my humble beginning, I did get promoted to a Senior Analyst after two years at Kaiser. My role switched from a technical focus to a project management focus. Being a first-time manager, I made my share of mistakes, but I learned from them. One of my earliest mistakes was assuming that a co-worker who did not ask questions understood how to do the analysis. She definitely did not, and I had to redo the analysis to meet the project deadline. I realized later that in my explanation of the very familiar analysis, I had left out some of the intermediate steps, assuming they were obvious. I learned to be more patient and more thorough in my explanations, as different people have different capacities for learning new skills. During my years as a Senior Analyst, I also learned from my boss what I did not want to be. This boss tended to shade the truth when it served him well. I believe honesty is the best policy.

After two years as a Senior Analyst, all on the same project, I longed for a change and took a job as a Financial Analyst for the Medical Group Administration at Kaiser's Los Angeles Medical Center. I managed the annual development of the budget (payroll and non-payroll) and enjoyed the opportunity to broaden my functional expertise. I also enjoyed the faster pace at the Medical Center compared to the Regional Offices. As in the past, I learned from my boss a characteristic I did not want to emulate: setting a double standard for herself and her staff. Ironically, during this time, I was first exposed to the principles of frontline leadership, and one of them was to lead by example.

Meanwhile, I hoped to enhance my career opportunities by networking my way into a Department Administrator position. I had daily access to several Assistant Medical Group Administrators, the Medical Group Administrator, and powerful physicians and department administrators. I learned several characteristics from these leaders that I hoped to emulate. They were on top of details, decisive, held their ground on their decisions, and were tough negotiators. Because I respected them, I sought ample career advice, asking how to move into line management. Their answer: there is no "right" path. Having a non-clinical (e.g., medical records, information systems, etc.) background did not necessarily preclude one's career advancement to the higher levels of clinical management. Many of the Assistant Medical Group Administrators admitted that they got where they were partly by luck; they were in the right place at the right time—not a very comforting thought to an aspiring MBA who wanted a "career path" formula to follow.

After two years in the Financial Analyst position, I was finishing up my MBA at UCLA's Fully Employed MBA Program. I became frustrated by at the fact that Kaiser seemed to be biased toward hiring those with a clinical background into Department Administrator positions; the business experience seemed to count less. I also watched several non-Kaiser employees become Kaiser employees in Department Administrator positions I aspired to. My MBA added credibility to my experience and opened up doors outside of Kaiser to me.

Although I was in the recruiting cycle at Deloitte & Touche, one of the Big 6 Consulting firms, I chose to take a Senior Financial Analyst position with Holy Cross Health System's Saint Agnes Medical Center in, of all places, Fresno, California. At the time, it seemed like a great opportunity. I hoped to be a "big fish in a little pond" and was led to believe by the executive search firm that I had a great chance for a promotion and $20,000 raise within six months. It cost less to live in Fresno, and the life style was slower. I was looking for a change of pace after three years of working full-time and going to business school. The Saint Agnes position turned out to be a real eye opener. I managed the budget process, as well as two exempt staff, and learned about several types of health insurance. At Kaiser, all I knew about was health maintenance organizations (HMOs). I picked up some valuable technical expertise in the area of hospital reimbursement and contractual allowances. I also learned that the rest of the health care world outside of Kaiser had different incentives; Saint Agnes wanted to keep its beds full, whereas Kaiser lost money if that happened.

After six months in the Senior Financial Analyst position and much frustration trying to supervise a CPA when I did not have the technical expertise to do so, I transferred to the Strategic Planning Department at Saint Agnes. I longed to get away from the "bean counting" in Financial Planning and manage projects with a broader business perspective. As a manager, I pushed the limits of my technical skills; I was making maps, programming and doing systems analyst work on huge databases, as well as pushing the limits of every piece of Microsoft software. I hated it. The job became a political nightmare, and I would not want to emulate my bosses. They were demeaning, dictatorial, and overly self-confident. They had a different perception of my abilities than my clients, and I could not succeed no matter how much I learned nor how much I tried. When I realized I was in a "no win" situation, I negotiated time to look for a new job, and began what one of my former colleagues referred to as my "12 Step Recovery Process" from my experience in Strategic Planning.

Present

I returned to Kaiser Permanente in the Sales and Marketing Department as a Project Manager in Market Services where I also supervise two analytical staff. I love my new bosses, both of whom I had worked with in my prior positions in Management Engineering at Kaiser, and I am currently learning a great deal from them about how to be a better manager. My Director has a great way of asking without imposing, perhaps because she asks her staff to do assignments with such confidence. Both my Director and my manager (my immediate boss) give me a lot of freedom to be creative. They are both very supportive of me; when I need a little political backing to implement a new initiative, they are right there beside me. This is such a contrast to my nightmare in Strategic Planning at St. Agnes Medical Center, where my immediate boss was actively trying to undermine my career.

Since I have been at Kaiser in my new role, I have also received some great advice from peers about how to be a better manager. One of my new employees is a long-term Kaiser worker, and she is not the "sharpest tack in the box." Needless to say, I have been frustrated with her lack of performance on several occasions, and have felt like venting to others. I have learned to be more careful about who I vent to, and one of my peers reminded me of the importance of being careful about who I open up to. She is reinforcing the lesson I learned so long ago at the Management Engineering lunch table at Kaiser.

In my current role as a Project Manager, I am learning some critical management skills because my job demands that I do in order to be effective. As Clint Patterson notes in his chapter on the value of an MBA, I have found that the people skills are so much more important to my success than any technical skill. As a Project Manager in a department that supports the direct sales force at Kaiser, I often must influence others to do things when these others are not my direct reports. Team building, guidance, and coaching are critical skills. I must also diffuse conflicts between departments by focusing on the issues, not on the people (another principle of frontline leadership). Rather than pointing the finger at our Information Services Department when something goes wrong with one of our direct mail campaigns, I must keep in mind that the business lines often have unrealistic turnaround times and still expect perfection. Additionally, I am learning what an important skill listening is. So many misunderstandings between departments could be avoided if people just listened to one another! I also find that my employees require some "venting" time each week; by listening, I show that I am concerned about their work life, and I try to offer constructive suggestions on how to deal with frustrating people, issues, etc.

Additional skills that are critical to being a good manager include perseverance, time management, passion for your work, and a broad base of experience. It is important that managers follow up on assignments that are delegated, especially to those who do not report directly to them. Perseverance is critical when you feel frustrated that your project is not being completed as quickly or easily as it should be. Time management is critical: there is too much to do in a day, and you have to be able to prioritize, especially when you have less staff than you did in the past. Luckily, business school was great preparation—professors deliberately assigned too much work, so that the students had to learn what was critical for success in the class and what was merely nice to know. Additionally, I could not work all the hours I do if I did not thoroughly enjoy what I do. As a manager, you have to have a passion for what you do and enjoy those you work with. The day goes so much faster as a result. Finally, a broad base of experience is essential to being a good manager: you have a much richer perspective if you have background in several functional areas. You can approach problems from a variety of angles, not just the same old way. Having an analytical background allows me to diffuse emotional arguments; it is hard to argue in the face of objective evidence to the contrary. I have also found the experience of working for different organizations to be enlightening. The rest of the health care world does not function like Kaiser!

Future

What does my future hold? I aspire to advance up the health care corporate ladder, obtaining managerial positions of increasing responsibility (i.e., bigger budget, bigger staff). I have not narrowed my career path to the support departments. If the opportunity presents itself, I may still try a clinical management career. I also definitely have not ruled out a career in consulting. I have avoided consulting in the past, because I feared I could not be successful and have a balanced life. I believe that a balance between work, family, personal, and spiritual life are key to the long-term success of any manager. However, as I become a better manager of my time, I have greater confidence in my ability to prioritize and achieve balance despite a hectic work schedule.

My dream is to reach the upper echelons of executive management in health care. Whether that means being a partner in a consulting firm or a CEO of a large HMO or other health care company remains to be seen. When I get there, I can say "I've made it!"

Managed Care Physician

Joe Spooner, MD, MBA

In 1983 I found myself in the midst of what was to be later called the "Managed Care Revolution." At the time, I was in private practice in Neurology on the Westside in Los Angeles. The Chairman of the Department of Neurology at UCLA, where I had trained, had asked me in 1981 if I wanted to manage the neurology teaching clinics, while I was growing my practice. I agreed as I was anxious to improve the clinics where I had trained and I was offered a helpful stipend to do so. However, I was also asked to sit on the CEO's Kitchen Cabinet of the UCLA Neuropsychiatric Hospital where our clinics and inpatient services were located. The Kitchen Cabinet was charged with finding a way to respond to a recent change in the way MediCal (California's Medicaid program) was to be paid for. The state of California, frustrated with the cost of MediCal, appointed a "MediCal Czar," named Mr. William Guy from Blue Cross, to oversee the process of change. MediCal, for the first time ever, was to contract out to hospitals. Price was to be the main factor in the negotiations. This meant that some hospitals that had routinely cared for MediCal patients, such as UCLA, could be excluded from admitting MediCal patients.

Today, it is routine for a payer, such as government or a private insurer, to contract for both hospital or physician care. But in the early 1980s, this change hit California healthcare like a tidal wave hitting a city. Although later euphemistically called the Managed Care Revolution, I believe we are still in what I call a Contracting Revolution. A true Managing Care Revolution is yet to come.

Medicare was also moving away from "cost plus" reimbursement, putting further pricing pressures on hospitals. I found myself in hospital budget meetings debating how we could lower staffing costs and lengths of stay. Physicians and healthcare administrators watched as over the next couple of years the private insurers became emboldened in their contracting for hospital and physician services. I recall early efforts by a few prescient UCLA faculty to put together a united medical group to negotiate with payers, and the anger this effort generated. Few knew how significant the changes were going to be in the way we practiced medicine over the next 10 years.

By the late 1980s I was anxious to be a major physician player in what was becoming the "business of medicine." The CEO of the UCLA Medical Center was the most senior physician executive I knew at the time so that was the position to which I aspired. I wanted to have an impact on the hospital's response to this change in healthcare financing and organization. I sought the counsel of a senior executive at Scripps in La Jolla, who advised me that the best next career step was to obtain an MBA degree. Without it, he advised, decision-makers in healthcare would not take me seriously; they would "only" see me in the role of a physician everyone stereotyped as someone incapable of balancing a checkbook, much less manage an institution. Even the physician CEO at UCLA told me with great conviction that "physicians don't know how to manage." Since that time I have heard this belief repeated by other physician executives, as if only they were gifted to manage, and all other physicians should be practicing!

In 1987 I started the Executive MBA program at UCLA with 55 other business people, and one other physician. Being immersed in business courses with business people is like going to medical school as an English major with 55 other doctorates in Zoology. But I would not have had it any other way, and I would be wary of any MBA program catering only to physicians. The best business school program teaches business to business people, and you are the lucky doctor who gets a chance to learn with them. The one exception I take to this statement is that it is helpful from the get-go to have formerly learned something about the healthcare financing and payment methods, such as capitation. An elective in the School of Public Health might accomplish that task.

Upon graduation, do not assume that everyone in managed care will appreciate all the work you put in to get an MBA degree. The President of CIGNA Healthcare of California at the time told me one day, "I don't have an MBA, why do you need one?" I was told by one chief medical officer at another company who turned me down as an associate, that he was threatened by what I knew, and wondered if he shouldn't get an MBA too. I eventually stopped putting "MBA" after my MD on my cards and correspondence.

However, having the knowledge that an MBA brought me has been invaluable in making my work more enjoyable and understandable on a day to day basis. It has definitely helped me be an effective physician executive. There are few business type activities, be they budgeting, facility planning, marketing, and, damn the words, "reorganizing" and "rightsizing," where some MBA course or courses have not been invaluable to me.

I must warn the reader that the latter two events, reorganizations and rightsizings (read layoffs) will affect you if you remain in managed care. I have seen presidents, CFOs, and chief medical officers come and go. I have played key roles in reorganization strategies that have laid off hundreds of employees in order to make "headcount' (a term I did not learn in business school but is heavily used in corporate environments). I have been affected on more than one occasion by reorganizations. In one instance, our company acquired a failing company, and two medical directors of the acquired company were let go. The remaining medical director, with only a few years of practice or managed care experience, and no MBA, replaced me, presumably at a lower salary than what my background had brought to the table. I was severed "without cause," affirmed that I did a fine job (I had never been told otherwise), and offered a severance package after negotiation. In the end, unless you really believe it is personal, you should never take a layoff as such, but as part of the business that has unfortunately become medicine, and as an opportunity to move on to better things.

Managed care is clearly a risky business for medical directors. Several reasons are evident: there are more and more doctors entering the medical director pool; medical directors are among the highest salary expenses to a company or group and are likely targets in cost control efforts; as medical directors train doctors to be more proactive utilizers there will be less need for traditional medical directors except in "denial" cases; mergers and acquisitions will reduce the number of medical directors needed; and chief medical officers generally take their orders from finance as to how many medical directors they can hire or keep (that is, the bottom line will often prevail).

Thus, one should never believe that layoffs would only affect others or only occur in failing companies. From the selfsame well that increased the need for more business savvy and full time medical directors, comes the pain of outsourcing, downsizing and reorganizing to make quarterly profit targets. This fact of life is particularly evident in more "mature" managed care markets like San Diego, LA and San Francisco. In younger markets, medical directors are in demand, particularly from managed care states like California. It is foolish to become a medical director and leave the practice of medicine as an escape measure. You must love being a manager first and relish the risk.

It is imperative that you seek a written employment contract from your employer that includes a reasonable severance package, and clear instructions as to what options there are, should there be a change of ownership or management upheaval. Physicians are particularly vulnerable and naive in the area of employment agreements and expectations. I recommend that MBA programs offer at least a one-day workshop on employment contract writing and negotiation taught by human resource and legal professionals.

In the 14 years I have been in managed care I have served in three different types of environments: I was a clinical director at the academic hospital and clinic level for 7 years, a senior level medical director at a large staff model HMO for 5 years, and for 2 years was a medical director of three IPAs in different geographic areas in California for a physician practice management company (PPM). Both the staff model and IPA positions were with publicly traded national companies.

What I learned in business school was just as relevant in the not-for-profit arena of academia, as it was for the for-profit companies. Success in operations, organizational design, budgeting, finance, human resources, and strategic planning, in this extremely resource-limited environment, is very important in the not-for-profit sector. There is little room for error anymore in either sector.

My first success in operations occurred on an academic ward where we employed total quality management techniques and saved $600,000 in one year through reduction of unnecessary bed days. I did this while still a student in Dr. Bill Yost's Operations class in the UCLA MBA program in 1988, and I attribute Bill's teaching for my inspiration to try out such techniques with faculty and residents.

By the time I finished the MBA program in 1989, I was anxious to get on with my goal of becoming a CEO of a hospital, so I interviewed in several places with that goal in mind. However, my friend and MBA compatriot, Dr. Deborah Shlian, had just left UCLA and had struck out on her own as a physician executive recruiter. She encouraged me to consider interviewing at CIGNA Healthcare where they were looking for a Regional Medical Director. My last interview before accepting that position was with a CEO of a hospital who was looking for a Chief Operating Officer. He was interested in me but what he said compelled me to go to CIGNA instead. He indicated that the hospital chain that owned his hospital treated it as a "cost center" and did not feel he needed his own CFO and other executives. This CEO felt controlled from the central office and was clearly not happy. He has since become a very successful and quoted CEO of another hospital system in a different part of the state. I still believe I made the correct choice by going the managed care route, but I sometimes wonder if that CEO had been happier when I talked with him, whether my career would have turned out differently.

In 1990, while at CIGNA Healthcare, I set-up Patient Flow Teams in 12 of our healthcare centers spread out across Los Angeles. We taught these teams to employ TQM and Theory of Constraints methodologies that I had learned at UCLA. The Patient Flow teams were successful at improving service and lowering cost per patient encounter. The late 80's and early 90's were periods of great corporate interest in TQM and I believed that I had found the perfect match of what I had learned in business school, my interest and talents and a healthcare system that needed my help. But another lesson was learned within a few years: the short time horizon for businesses driven by the quarterly report. Even the best of ideas in business, such as TQM, will be discarded if the benefits do not seem immediate, or the new senior management (and every 2 years it is usually new) has no interest in it.

By 1993, CIGNA Healthcare was downsizing and reorganizing for the second time in 2 years. Employees feared the so-called "re-engineering" team that came from the corporate office on the East Coast because their visits always resulted in layoffs; the quality guru hired by the president left and TQM was dead. Unknown to most employees the CIGNA Medical Group, a staff model that was once Ross-Loos, the oldest HMO in the country, was being dressed for market, and was later sold to Caremark International. CIGNA had decided it no longer wanted to manage employed physicians.

I left CIGNA after another desperate reorganization and 6 months before the CIGNA Medical Group was acquired by Caremark International. Rather than enlist the medical leadership of the CIGNA Medical Group, Caremark made the mistake of utilizing the leadership of a nearby group that it had earlier purchased. Right out of the classic business school case came the difficulty of merging two medical groups that had widely disparate cultures. The CIGNA Medical Group, a proud group with roots back to 1929, felt it was being managed by a group that was medically and managerially inferior. Transition management had failed.

Caremark itself was later acquired by MedPartners/Mullikan, a large Physician Practice Management Group (PPM). Ironically, Mullikan had been a competitor group to the CIGNA Medical Group in Los Angeles for many years.

By 1995 I had worked in managed care in an academic setting and with a staff model. I then accepted a medical director position with a newly public physician practice management company (PPM), FPA Medical Management of San Diego, to manage 3 newly acquired IPA's from Foundation Health. Like CIGNA with its medical group in LA, Foundation had had its hands full managing these IPAs whose medical loss ratios had reached 130%. Foundation Health jumped at the chance to sell off the IPAs. It later sold the Foundation Health staff model to FPA as well. By this transaction, Foundation Health was, in essence, outsourcing its risk in provider costs to a physician-founded PPM, on the assumption that FPA could better manage physicians. Indeed, we were able to reduce the medical loss ratio down of these troubled IPAs to about 80% in the first year. Initially, the physicians in the IPAs were happy to see a PPM that had been "founded by physicians."

PPMs such as FPA and MedPartners will play an increasing role in managed care for the next several years. The PPM experience was enjoyable and personally rewarding; however, FPA underutilized my business background and experience and I was getting restless. FPA wanted a less experienced physician, at less compensation, who was satisfied in a more traditional medical director's role; and, I believe an MBA from a good business school prepares you for more than a traditional utilization management, rubber-stamping quality management position. The latter is fine for entry-level medical director positions: one has to pay one's dues, but you should move on if you are not appreciated for what your background brings to the table.

I envision PPMs as another transition model towards what I call "Community-based supra-IPAs." These supra-IPA's will bring physicians in the communities back together, that the divisive contract strategies by different healthplans have separated in the last 10 years. These supra IPAs will negotiate directly with local employers and individuals for care. It is at this level where I believe the MBA-educated physician leader will be most valued by managed care players. The bureaucracies of the PPMs and the Healthplans will be less and less effective at cost control and patient satisfaction as physician groups and individual practitioners get the hang of managing care to cost and quality. Astute medical directors with experience and MBAs will be retained to head up these organizations, in my view, and will play key roles in developing networks, and leading negotiation with employers, educating them and their employees in what medical value really is. Medical value is not just another contract with another group at a lower price.

Another value of an MBA degree is the ability to move within the medical business environment, comfortable that you can succeed. I am currently President and CEO of Impact Medical Technology, a medical marketing company. I have found that vendors in the medical marketplace can benefit from the insights of an experienced medical director in the development and execution of their business plans. I should know; I have sat on the other side of vendors' presentations for 14 years.

MANAGED CARE PHYSICIAN EXECUTIVE

Charles Payton, MD, MBA

Understand Your Mission: Medical School

I entered medical school in 1967, in the midst of an era of student activism. My class was filled with students demanding relevance in the curriculum and a demonstration of community sensitivity. I felt a strong pull to these goals and with the enthusiasm of my classmates I took on the role of organizer of early clinical experiences, community health symposia, and as an elected spokesperson for student organizations. Following my sophomore year I participated in a summer program in Washington D.C. known as the Institute for the Study of Health and Society. During this three-month program I had contact with many of the significant health care leaders and academicians of the time. I had an opportunity to work with the Urban Coalition and one of its' subsidiaries known as the Health Manpower Development Corporation. I was able to establish a relationship with the director of Indian Health service, which led to a contract for placing health science students with Native American tribes in the Southwest. These programs gave me opportunities to develop skills in budgeting, negotiating, program planning and development. With this combination of local and national activities, I became national President of the Student American Medical Association (SAMA). I dealt regularly with the American Medical Association (AMA), the American Academy of Family Physicians (AAFP) and other national organizations negotiating public policy positions and representing student interests. As a medical student, I found myself speaking to the AMA, presenting to congressional committees, and talking to audiences of leaders in the insurance and pharmaceutical industries. While the reductionistic approach of medical school was forcing me to take an increasingly micro view of medicine, my experience with socio-political systems demonstrated how an individual could make a powerful an impact through organizational leadership.

Establish Your Competence: Residency

I entered a primary care residency following medical school with the commitment to establish my competence as a clinician. It seemed clear that within the medical community any attempt to be a leader would be predicated on achieving the intellectual and behavioral attributes of a successful practitioner. It wasn't entirely clear to me whether that assessment was to be rendered by the patient community or the professional peer community. Either way I wanted to establish my clinical qualities as a requisite to any direction I would take in the future. I continued to participate in a Foundation Board and a minority health manpower training corporation. I served as a chief resident during my third year seeing it as an opportunity to create cooperation between the faculty and the house staff to strengthen the program in several targeted areas. Passing my specialty boards gave me the affirmation that the competence I was striving for would be achieved.

Establish Your Credibility: Clinical Practice

In 1975 I joined two medical school friends to open a practice in a rural community of 1500. We were immediately challenged with the economics of a new practice in a community that had high seasonal unemployment, a migratory native American population and a Hill

Burton financed hospital which could not muster a census sufficient to operate in the black. I became the manager/director of the practice responsible for implementing a computerized business system, hiring a professional lay administrator, supervising the office staff, and making plans for the expansion of the practice. The practice eventually grew to six physicians, a nurse practitioner, physician assistant and a women's health care specialist. Having built an innovative group practice, my attention was turned to redeveloping the hospital facility as a comprehensive ambulatory care site with an emergency room, alternative birthing center, laboratory and radiology services. The plan, which was developed with extensive research, was predicated on the consolidation of patient services at a hospital less than five miles away but across the state line. Although the plan was well developed from a programmatic and financial standpoint, it was flawed on the political front. The public hospital board was not about to diminish the image of their community by losing a hospital and the associated commercial business to an adjacent community, particularly one across the state border. During this three year period I gained a great deal of knowledge and skill in the operation of a successful medical practice, but found out at the same time that political success may have little to do with the credibility that comes from managerial achievement.

Seek and Accept Accountability: Academic Medicine

After three years of practice, I joined the new departmental faculty of a medical school converting from a two-year basic science institution to a full four-year degree granting institution. I was given responsibility for directing the facility in which the entire faculty conducted private practice and the primary care residents received their continuity ambulatory training. The school was built on a commitment to use community practitioners as the major clinical teaching resource. Unfortunately, most of the clinicians (I later discovered) had not been consulted when the university developed its plan for the medical school. I wrote the residency accreditation documents and simultaneously convinced and cajoled practitioners to be a volunteer faculty. The school was so under resourced that I regularly felt I was responding to the mission with smoke and mirrors rather than leading the development of a high quality academic department. Never had I confronted such a challenge at an ethical level. This was the first time in my career I can recall spending sleepless nights which culminated in proffering my resignation in order to obtain the support needed to achieve and maintain accreditation for this program.

Recognize Your Constituency: Entrepreneurial Experiments

In 1978 I left my first academic position to assume the directorship of another university's Family Practice Residency. Soon after arriving, I was given the opportunity to start four unique community based practices. This venture developed in collaboration with a national hospital and nursing home company that was branching out into ambulatory care. This was my first opportunity to hire, manage and evaluate large numbers of physicians. I promoted (with the corporate partner) the value of a physician participation model, which created ownership or equity as a tool to stimulate productivity and customer satisfaction. What I confronted was a corporate culture that treated employees as costs rather than investments. A year of arm wrestling with national management led to my decision to withdraw from the venture. Within 18 months the firm discontinued this line of business and sold off all of its holdings. During the same time (1983-85) I presented a proposal to the Robert Wood Johnson foundation to develop an HMO to be owned and operated by my University. I developed a relationship with the Vice

President for Health Sciences who shared the vision that health maintenance organizations represented an inevitable paradigm shift in the financing and organization of health services. The grant was successful in the competitive cycle and the University received an award of $1.5 million to be used over three years to plan and implement an HMO that would enroll both commercial and Medicaid beneficiaries. The notion of providers assuming risk for the plan's financial performance was threatening however to the academic departments and the hospital administration. There were no models for such interdependence and each party felt vulnerable to the questionable performance of other partners. While trying to develop a basis for all of the academic departments to work in a way that would be mutually beneficial, the project confronted unexpected resistance from a key leader. The hospital CEO was also on the board of directors of the state's Blue Cross/Blue Shield Plan! He had no interest in seeing his institution create competition for the Blues. When the Vice President for Health Sciences left his position I lost the necessary internal advocate for the project to succeed.

Lay the Path to Your Goals

During these preceding years (1970 through 1985) I periodically considered the value of obtaining an advanced degree. I had known medical school classmates who obtained MPH concurrent with their MD degrees. The perspective they shared with me about their curriculum did not seem to address the challenges that I was most interested in. I recognized the need for more business training, as a resource in meeting my own organization's leadership expectations and as preparation for negotiation with health care purchasers. The many changes in my job situation over this time frame kept me from seeking a degree within either of the universities with which I was affiliated.

Stretch Yourself: The "Academic" Corporation

In 1985 I took the directorship of a Family Practice Residency in Southern California. During the recruiting process I negotiated an agreement with the hospital CEO that I would form a professional corporation to employ the faculty and contract with the hospital for the operation of the clinical practice and the administration and teaching of the residency. In my university residency directorships, I found the opportunities for innovation to be greatly constrained by bureaucratic structures. Of even more significance, was the fact that in negotiating for resources or policy changes, administrative rank was frequently more predictive of the outcome than was the virtue of the proposal. I wanted the new arrangement to free my organization from such encumbrances as management by a hospital billing and accounting office, personnel control through hospital human resources unit, and appointment of faculty based on the medical staff politics. Within the first 60 days I had set up a new corporation and drafted the contract with the hospital. I became the owner and president of the professional corporation, which was given the unique mission of being financially successful and balancing the evaluation of clinicians between productivity and scholarly performance. I spent five years building the faculty, putting sound practice management in place, redeveloping the curriculum around new training requirements and strengthened institutional affiliations. As I approached my twelfth year of academic employment, I felt that the problems and opportunities were being re-cycled without many new challenges. I needed new stimuli and the organization could benefit from a leader with a new set of ideas. Our hospital was part of an integrated delivery system that seemed to offer a number of career opportunities. Several positions were explored but none made good use of my experience and skills. It seemed that most had no clear path associated with them. In looking back, I realize that my notion of a career path was far too linear and anticipated an increase in span of responsibility with each step. In retrospect, many of the opportunities would have been good compliments to my previous training and would have allowed me to move about in the organization to gather the knowledge and skills. In the midst of this career search, I decided to attend one of the Physician in Management seminars put on several times a year by the American College of Physician Executives. During that weeklong program, three of the faculty said in similar ways if you are going to spend more than ten years of your career in administration/leadership, get an MBA. That was my catalyst for action! I went back to the residency, submitted applications to business schools and started succession planning. Within four months I was accepted to the Executive MBA at UCLA and had mapped out a process for the residency and hospital to appoint an interim director while completing a national search for my replacement.

Grant Yourself Rewards: The Masters Program

The first two quarters of the MBA covered subjects with which I was familiar. They were however approached with a new relevance and reestablished my skills in accounting, economics, and statistics. The finance courses were a new experience and one I didn't appreciate at the time. Having now dealt with mergers, acquisitions and startups, I have found the discipline to be extremely necessary. Marketing was a gas! I think it simultaneously touched my competitive drive and my reliance on statistics, even those derived from consumer surveys. The organizational strategy courses were excellent models for linking competitive planning to operational execution. The most indelible lessons were delivered by the faculty that taught from a systems perspective. They hammered home the lesson that successful companies are those that are continuously learning. They demonstrated the pursuit of evaluative information and the application of data analysis to modification, renovation and reinforcement of business strategies. I finished the EMBA with two clear conclusions. I had validated much of what I learned previously on the job and I had recognized how manufacturing and retail industries had lessons to be applied to the healthcare industry.

Create Opportunities: Running a Health Plan

Before I finished the EMBA, opportunities to look at new jobs opened up. I had always thought I was preparing for a position with a provider organization. When a search firm presented an opportunity at Blue Cross of California, I was unclear how my background and education would be applied in such an organization. I was equally clear however, that spending time working with a major payer would give me a circumspect view of the healthcare industry, which would be valuable in the future. In 1992 I took the position that was offered at Blue Cross initially working for the Corporate Medical Director who was a Senior Vice President. I felt my business skills were much stronger than his, but I soon recognized his contribution to the company was in an entirely different capacity. He was the spokesperson for the provider community's opinion and expectations. He had a keen sense of public accountability. He mentored me for several months and helped me learn the routines of that organization or rather the Blue Cross accumulation of organizations. Once I understand the Blue Cross culture and became familiar with it's structural realities, I was able to answer the question of how I could contribute to the organization and satisfy my own goals at the same time. The BCC organizations presented diverse business needs and unique managerial styles. Also, the organization undergoes a periodic metamorphosis creating many opportunities for career movement. I was able to spend a year and a half as the medical director of the company's PPO. In that position I learned utilization management, quality improvement, case management, underwriting and reimbursement methodologies. I then moved into a new area for the company as it developed its first business plan for Medicaid Managed Care. I was one of very few professionals in the company who had any knowledge of MediCal. My background gave me an opportunity to educate and train others while developing strategies that would be unique to the company. I performed direct provider contracting, training, and management. None of these had been part of the Blue Cross of California operating methodology. Based on my relationship with community practitioners, I was convinced that Blue Cross could become a true managed care company if it did more in the provider arena patterned after the pure HMOs such as FHP and PacifiCare. I proposed that BCC start providing MSO services as a line of business. I wrote white papers and met with senior management in an attempt to convince them of the potential value of investing resources in such a startup. Simultaneously, unanticipated market changes caused BCC to start two medical groups in counties along the central coast of California. It was necessary to have a physician owner for the Professional Corporations which operated the groups, and managerial leadership was needed for the MSOs which were built to support these groups. I left the MediCal division after a year and a half to take charge of the practices and network development in these two counties. This was for me the ultimate synthesis of my professional skills and organizational knowledge. I managed resources from all the major divisions of Blue Cross; actuarial, contracting, information systems, marketing, and human resources. At the same time Blue Cross was going through its failed merger with HSI/Healthnet and went on to purchase the healthcare businesses of Massachusetts Mutual and John Hancock. The scope and scale of the company's business changed dramatically with a doubling of beneficiaries and the introduction of multi-state business units. Not unpredictably, the company s focus moved further away from the provider community and diminished an already small interest in attempting to build a return on investment through operations of provider (professional or institutional) services. Much of my justification for promoting BCC's entry into the MSO business line was the need for the company to learn about the issues and preferences of the provider community which seemed necessary for Blue Cross to effectively partner with either physicians or hospitals. The flaw was in the assumption that I could ever interest Blue Cross in pursuing such partnerships. The ROI formula for that organization is a pure economic model. There was insufficient leadership in the company familiar with the delivery system to see a value in broadening the company's view of value creation for provider customers.

Know the Breadth of Your Business: The Integration (IDS) Model

The opportunity to use my practice management skills, my strategic planning ability, and my experience with health plan design and operations emerged in a position I assumed a year ago. I am the CEO and Medical Director of a Foundation model medical group. That foundation is part of a regionally focused 5-hospital system. In addition to the hospitals, the system owns an IPA, home health companies, a laboratory company, pharmacies, skilled nursing facilities and an ambulatory surgery center. In the last two years the growth and maturation of the IDS has focused on the physician strategy which is necessary to compete with other major providers in the area and begin building a new clinical paradigm. I have been able to apply all my experiences from directing capitation operations, establishing competent practice administration, budgeting and accounting, and human resource management. The varieties of lessons learned in prior jobs and in the EMBA program have allowed me to respond to the diverse needs of my organization and provide valuable assistance as the chief physician in this IDS. Our goal is the ultimate synthesis of the enterprise to competently manage the full spectrum of clinical services and do it successfully through full financial risk. With the acquisition of a limited HMO license and the opportunity to contract as a provider sponsored network we will accomplish both the ultimate justification and absolute necessity for designing and delivering a better model of healthcare!

INTEGRATED DELIVERY SYSTEM EXECUTIVE

Eleanor Brewer, MEd, MBA

> *Hold fast to dreams,*
> *for if dreams die,*
> *Life is a broken winged bird,*
> *that cannot fly.*
> *—Langston Hughes*

Values in Action…

How does one adequately reflect back on so many years and so many people and experiences which have influenced one's life? For me, it is with thanks and with gratefulness. Thanks to people I know and have known, thanks to being at the right place at the right time, thanks to being ready when the right time came, and thanks to a reasoned view of success.

As I write this I am the Vice President of Research & Development at a health system that has moved to become an integrated delivery system. The legal and financial linking of the continuum of care components has taken the focus and energies of numerous members of our executive teams. The organizations which have been linked together can all be classified in the top of their fields whether they are hospitals, physicians, home health agencies, ambulatory care facilities or others. The challenge that continues to lie before us is the linking of care between these facilities so that we provide that seamless care our customers desire with a coordinated focus on the patient and family.

A further challenge to us is to be able to leverage our many and varied capabilities in carrying out our mission of continuously improving the health and quality of life of people in the communities in which we serve. This is the challenge for the R & D department as well as the more than 20,000 caring people who make up our organization.

These challenges continue to motivate and inspire me. Actually, as I think back, virtually every move that I have made in my career came as a result of a passion for something I valued. When I believe in something, I act on it. The process of moving causes forward has not only furthered the cause, but also unintentionally furthered my career. What a wonderful opportunity in life to be able to act on one's ideals and, as an unexpected byproduct, reap career rewards. I never planned this life. Who could have? But, it suits me just fine. Please let me explain the gratefulness I feel and the causes which have moved me forward.

Although not from a broken home, I lived winters in an idyllic rural village and summers in a bustling, exciting cosmopolitan center. The virtue of spending my early years in two diverse geographic areas was to make me totally comfortable in either setting conversing with people about anything from farm prices to Broadway plays. It has also enabled me to truly experience the current moment, wherever I am, without longing to be somewhere else.

My earliest motivations came from my father and mother who placed high value on getting an education, understanding that life is not always easy, and that by the luck of the draw I was born to middle-class parents who provided a stable home and a comfortable, interesting life. This latter point is significant in that I was taught to believe that it was luck that I had this life and not that I was due this life. As a result, it was made clear to me to give to others who did not have the luck I had.

My tendency to stand up for causes also began at home. My father was a town councilman and worked constantly to improve life in our village. As an electrician, he provided free services for the elderly and the poor, particularly elderly women who had no one to do those many tasks in a home that was aging along with them. My mother was a supporter of the schools, a girl scout leader, a homemaker, and an advocate for justice for all. She preached against the unfairness of racial inequality and the plight of the poor. Mom will long be remembered for stopping joke tellers in their tracks when it came to ethnic slurs. She was Polish by birth and was quick to call anyone to task who told a "Polish" joke around her. She politely, but firmly asked how they would like the same joke told with their ethnicity inserted. The laughter was always cut short and the conversation moved to a higher plane immediately.

The war in Vietnam was firmly supported in our village, but not by my parents. They were early, outspoken critics of the government movement of troops into Vietnam, of the horror of the nightly body counts, and viewed with great skepticism the explanations spilling forth from Washington to justify these actions. As a family we were united in our opposition. Father was a World War II veteran of both the South American and European theaters, but he and mother were part of the first voices that sounded like whispers and later became the roar of an enraged country.

My higher education began with a degree from a private women's college. This is only noteworthy since graduating from a rural high school I was one of only two women in my class to go on to receive a college degree. Most assumed their roles as wives and mothers in our village.

At that time there were about thirty colleges and universities in the United States which offered a Bachelor's degree in Medical Record Administration. I had figured out that upon graduation this degree led to an instant department head position. In fact, I became the youngest department director ever when, following my husband to a new city during a position transfer for him, I joined a major medical center.

During these early years of my career I found great value in knowing and interacting with others in my profession. And in fact, because of being active in my professional organization I had my new position well in advance of my husband's transfer to that new city and state. In these professional organizations I rose through the ranks of committee member to chairman and eventually to president. In the process I met many interesting and talented people who to this day I can call my friends and colleagues. I was energized by a pride in my profession and vision of it having the mission of providing access to medical information to patients and improving the quality of care. In those years patients were not allowed to see their medical records and many were never told their diagnoses. We were a paternalistic industry at that time, protecting people from the knowledge that they had a terminal disease with the mistaken belief that it would be too much for them to handle and that they wouldn't understand the medical language and implications. These pervasive beliefs angered and infuriated me.

About that time I gave birth to a beautiful baby girl and we stopped referring to ourselves as a couple and proudly took on the new designation of family. My husband was again transferred and our little family moved to a new city and a new home. The move gave me the opportunity to complete a Masters in Education while teaching as a full-time assistant professor in the school of allied health at the university medical school.

After a few years, a new hospital building began to appear on the horizon near where we lived and I decided to leave the familiarity of the university and take the risk of starting something entirely new. It was a shell of a building when I was hired as employee number five and the following year was spent building the medical staff, the systems infrastructure, and the clientele for that new institution.

While serving as the president of my state's professional association, I learned of a movement by the state legislature to begin collecting patient information to be used for multiple undefined purposes. I became concerned about the privacy of individuals and armed with my training around the confidentiality of patient records pursued unrelentingly to become a part of the decision making body of that movement. After numerous phone calls and much lobbying on my part I was invited to a meeting chaired by the Representative of a neighboring legislative district who had been chosen by the Governor to lead this effort.

I had gotten my wish. There I was in a room full of the movers and shakers of health care for my state. Present were the president of the hospital association, the head of the state Center for Health Statistics, the president of the medical society, the president of the nurses association, the president of the largest PSRO in the United States, the list went on and on. And then there was me, feeling strong willed, indignant and like a bumpkin among giants.

Soon after I had arrived at the meeting the Representative asked me to leave the room with him for a minute, at which point he asked me to chair the committee he had assembled! Not knowing what I was getting into or why he had selected me, I said yes thinking he probably wouldn't ask twice. I figured I knew Robert's Rules of Order, there was an agenda to follow, and why not? So off we marched back into that room. A dead silence fell on the room as he announced my chairmanship. Then came the uninhibited protests of the members. But the Representative was steadfast and I called the meeting to order.

It was much later that I learned why I had been selected to chair that influential committee. I was the only person present who's total agenda was the protection of the right to privacy of the individual patient. The hospital association was concerned about the disclosure of information relative to hospitals. The president of the medical society was even more concerned about the disclosure of individual physician data. On and on it went with each faction advocating to either release more or less data depending upon their constituency. In the 1970s this was a forerunner to the data bases that are present in many states today. To give you a quick end to the story, patients were not identifiable and I became part of the executive committee of the organization.

As a result of speaking out publicly so many times on behalf of patients, I was offered many positions by the members of my committee and eventually joined the state's hospital association. This moved involved some risk, since there was no clearly defined position for me.

It wasn't long before I was put in charge of developing a $9 million corporate headquarters for the Association. The project was a success in its meeting the needs of the organization and in having been completed ahead of schedule and under budget. The resulting 60,000 square foot office building stood quietly hidden on 22 acres of land. Though located along a major business research corridor it was nominated for an architectural award for its design and for preserving the virgin forest on the land. We were rewarded with the return of the deer and animals that came up to our windows and looked in on us as we pursued the weighty issues of health care. What a calming effect those beautiful creatures had on us.

My role continued to expand to working with the Professional Standards Review Organizations (PSROs), lobbying, and, of course, advocating. This time advocating for physicians to have input into hospital association activities. I saw us as partners, not enemies and felt more informed decisions could be made by bringing the physician voice into the discussion. With that I was asked to start the first Medical Staff Council and the input process began. By now I was a vice president at the hospital association and an adopted nine year old boy was added as our son.

A few years passed and the association's president left to assume the leadership a large health system on the West Coast owned by a beautiful congregation of religious Sisters. After nine months of convincing presidential rhetoric and with the encouragement of my husband, we moved our family to join my former president in his new work. I became the Vice President "of Other Things." The system I had joined was a new health system, not a new system of hospitals, but rather a newly incorporated umbrella organization. Opportunities abounded.

So much needed to be done so that these hospitals and allied businesses, which were already outstanding in their singularity, could be even more outstanding in their "systemness". The Sisters, who for almost 75 years had been meeting the needs of the insured and the uninsured alike in their communities, were aging. The number of young women joining religious orders had gone from a torrent to a trickle. It was soon apparent to this congregation of women that they needed to build a new infrastructure which continued to be based upon a mission of service, but carried out by lay people and not dependent upon Sister leadership.

Tapping into my previous building experience, my first responsibility was the creation of a corporate office building. After many meetings with the surrounding neighborhoods and zoning changes I built a new, more modern home to house the novices, the women preparing to join the order. Having relocated the previous occupants I was then able to remove the total insides of an existing building down to the beam structure and recreate it from the novices' home and high school to a corporate headquarters. Its location on the Motherhouse property near a spectacular lawn and rose garden gave it a unique setting among corporations.

As the headquarters construction proceeded I began work on the creation of a malpractice and general liability insurance company to serve the needs of our diverse organization. Openly asking questions, pursuing information from experts and studying the subtleties of the business I was able to gain the knowledge needed to form this new business entity. My goal was to not only create an insurance company for the present, but to create a business which, when viewed many years after its inception, would be seen as a strategic asset for the corporation rather than a tangle of poorly conceived business decisions. Located off shore, it became a full-fledged insurance company which could write policies for our own as well as for other commercial businesses.

The most challenging part of the development of an insurance company is obtaining reinsurance—which is that portion of risk sold to others who will in turn become responsible for the exposure. Insurance executives speak of utmost good faith when referring to risk disclosure. That is, the disclosure of all the known issues around the risk to be insured. It was on this principle and our reputation that we were able to attract the preeminent reinsurer in the United States to provide occurrence coverage at a reasonable premium with an agreement of moderated premium fluctuations. The success of this company can be seen today as it returns millions of dollars of premiums to our individual insured businesses because of excellent claims experience and a risk management system build upon the philosophy of prevention, immediate disclosure, and honesty to those involved.

With the new building occupied by an ever growing number of corporate people and the insurance company staffed and covering our various businesses, the headlines on the nightly news reported an earthquake in neighboring Mexico City. Later we would learn that the earthquake registered 8.1 on the Richter scale. It lasted only 4 minutes but claimed 5,000 lives, and an additional 30,000 people were injured and 40,000 were left homeless. Damage to property topped $3 billion. The call came late that night from our company president asking me to lead a team of people from our system to help the people of Mexico. What to do? I didn't speak Spanish. I had never been to Mexico let alone been in an earthquake or seen the effects of its devastation. Calls to the United States State Department and many relief organizations received instant replies when the million dollars of aid we were prepared to give were mentioned.

What was the problem then? Just give the money to these organizations and get on with the day-to-day activities that were happening so fast at the Health System. Deep down, I knew that wouldn't do. That the people I was representing would want to know how the funds were used, who they helped, how we decided to maximize the help this money could bring. So no, I couldn't just send a check. Soon a team had been assembled to make a needs assessment trip to Mexico City.

This adventurous little band consisted of the director of Central Supply at one of our hospitals who had grown up in Mexico City and another gentleman who also spoke Spanish and was in charge of one of our largest pharmacies. The final member of the team was one of our communication directors. The Red Cross met them at the airport and soon they were touring the destruction in ambulances. In a city of 17 million people, Mexico City is a perpetual traffic jam in all directions and the use of ambulances made it possible to move somewhat quickly through the city.

Normal communications were down between our two countries, but soon a call via short wave radio arrived as the home team of purchasing directors stood by with me to receive the news of where the greatest needs were. Twelve story Juarez hospital, the city's largest, had fallen crushing hundreds of people. Immediate emergency response came from around the world, but the task of rebuilding the world's most populous city required a more sustained effort. The loss of Juarez Hospital jeopardized the future care of people and closed a major education site for medical students and allied health professionals. The needs were read carefully and clearly over the tenuous radio connection. Sixty gurneys, five anesthetic machines, multiple portable x-ray units, four surgical tables, crash carts, the list of needs grew longer and longer. A time was set for them to call the next morning after our purchasing team was able to determine from our many vendors and manufacturers the availability of the necessary equipment.

When we spoke again that next day receiving an affirmative to the total list, we could hear the cries of relief and excitement of the Mexican health care workers in the background. The equipment that was sent was all new and arrived with teams of people to help install it and instruct in its operation. Major manufacturers teamed with us to give best prices or even no price at all and to ask their customers who were in line to have items shipped to agree to a delay so that we could ship the newly available pieces to help the people of Mexico. It ended up being the efforts of hundreds of known and still unknown people who made a significant contribution to rebuilding the health care facilities and educational infrastructure which had so quickly been ripped away that one September day. I only set off the spark and good hearts of the people carried it to conclusion. The Archbishop of Mexico City led a mass in honor of our Health System and the plaque of appreciation at the Red Cross Hospital remains to this day. Also, there remains a lasting bond between our organization and the Cruz Roja of Mexico City. Physicians have come to our hospitals to learn new medical techniques and we continue to share supplies and expertise.

Back to running our insurance company: I was by this time almost done with my Master of Business Administration from UCLA. Our health system continued to grow and had recently purchased a health maintenance organization. Although the HMO was losing money, we saw it as a strategic move to expand our business. Recognizing our forte at the time was to operate hospitals, an experienced HMO management firm was hired to run the company. Within our first year of ownership, the membership grew from 23,000 members to 63,000 members, but systems needed to support that growth were not in place. The money losses went from six to seven digits on a monthly basis with no relief in sight. To add to the pending crisis the federal qualification of the HMO was now in jeopardy.

The call came late one Friday after I had arrived home from school. The president had arranged for the executive staff of the HMO to meet with me the next morning to do a rapid turn around of the tenuous federal qualification. The site visit by federal inspectors which had ended earlier that day had left us with a list of deficiencies which extended for pages and covered everything from member services to finances. Why me? Why call me? I don't even know what an HMO is. I knew we bought one, but that was all. I had homework to do. My children had homework to do. I needed a haircut.

When I arrived the next morning the HMO staff members were nervous and demoralized. They had taken a beating in the past week that removed any spirit they had left to do their jobs. Imagine their delight to see someone arrive from the corporate office who was now going to give orders. Beleaguered as they were, they rose to the occasion and in a week we had produced more than thought humanly possible and, holding our collective breaths, we shipped the documentation off to Washington for a ruling.

A month of suspense ensued during which time I went back to running our insurance company and catching up on family and homework. Then, another call came from the president. Washington was granting us the requested extra time to finish the corrections and make the systemic changes. About four months later spring arrived along with my graduation and an inspection team from Washington. We were all spit and polish with our new infrastructures in place when Washington confirmed what we had known: the federal qualification was retained as well as extended into additional service areas.

Soon, a new president was hired for the HMO and I was asked to stay on as part of the executive team. This time my title was Senior Vice President and I was now responsible for member services, employer group services and renewals, government relations, legal, human resources, and facilities. The HMO president kept the company focused on the basics and in less than two years our incredible losses became minor net incomes and by five years the company was at the top of its game. Net income moved into eight digits. Membership had grown to 125,000, loss ratios and overhead were meeting or exceeding industry standards and the resulting profitability put the company at a decision point.

In order to continue to be competitive in the expanding managed care market, it would be necessary to grow the company at a faster pace. To accomplish this, Health System capital dollars would be needed to purchase other HMOs to be merged with our company. At that moment in time the corporation president left to lead a national system of hospitals and we had new leadership at the top of our Health System.

At the end of our Health System deliberations on the future of our HMO we realized that the appetite for capital by acute health care facilities was, at that time, too great to support a huge diversion of capital funds to support sufficient growth for our HMO business. A sale of the HMO to a values-based and much larger HMO was soon negotiated. Based upon our Sisters' view of employee work life, significant portions of the negotiation concerned what was to happen to the employees and how to minimize their traumas.

With the sale imminent I returned to the Health System corporate offices, this time as the Vice President of Quality. The continuous quality improvement (CQI) and total quality management (TQM) movements were sweeping health care and everyone was training and forming teams. Paradigm shifts, systems thinking, learning organizations, empowered employees, variation analysis, best practices and other exciting concepts were unfolding. So again I studied, read, listened and asked questions. I met Dr. W. Edwards Deming and to this day can hear his voice. The voice of a man with a vision and a deep conviction. I was deeply moved and the resulting knowledge made me think back wistfully to my HMO days when all the systems were tangled and unworkable. Had I known then what I knew now, life would have been much easier during the correction process.

The learning of the concepts of quality and the knowledge of our leadership and organization led to my recommending that we not form a major corporate center for quality. Rather, that the individual entities be supported in their efforts to further these concepts and systems at the local level within the context of the culture of each of our business entities. To begin the process, the executive leadership of the entities were brought together to learn and hear from others. The task remained then, to support their individual efforts whatever form these would take.

As my work moved into the world of voice mail, e-mail, computers at every work station and a dynamic explosion of communication capabilities took place, my children moved into their young adult lives. One moved on to higher education and the other took a job working at a residential facility for the severely disabled. At this point travel became more far reaching and rather than only for business it became the source of great pleasure and excitement for personal growth and enrichment. Tokyo, Paris, Corsica,

London, Rome, Helsinki, St. Petersburg, and many, many more became familiar places of multiple visits with an ever-expanding circle of friends.

My belief in the value of education began to play a greater role in my activities outside of health care. First, as President of UCLA's Executive MBA Alumni Association and, more recently, as President of UCLA's Anderson Alumni for the graduate school of management, I am called upon to speak publicly of the value of education and of the value of the people one meets in the process of gaining an education.

As I noted when I began this reflection, I'm now the Vice President of Research & Development having been asked to take on the creation of this department by the third and newest president of our Health System. His early career years had been spent with a mammoth world-wide consumer products company and were followed by many years of defining and implementing strategy in health care. He understands of the value of R & D in consumer products and is anxious to translate that into health services research for the betterment of the lives of people in our service communities.

The story is not over, but that is all there is to tell for the present. Except perhaps that grandchild number four is on the way. I hope the themes come to life for you, the reader. Education, strong beliefs in what is right, the desire to help others, the importance of family and friends, and a silly little memory of a girl scout rule of trying to leave every place better for your having been there. I haven't always been successful with what has happened on a day-to-day basis, but over time things have turned out rather well. My best wishes to readers on your achievements of success, however you define it, and even more that the joy of living predominates in your life.

INSURANCE COMPANY EXECUTIVE

Alan Bramson, MBA

My family consists almost entirely of academicians and scientists—my father was a PhD and engineer, my mother was a schoolteacher, and my brothers were physicians, chemists and mathematicians. I am the first and only one active in the business world. Although during my college days at Reed College I initially assumed I must follow in their footsteps and become a physician or chemist, reality quickly made me realize that these were not my interests, nor necessarily my strengths. After a few painful years dabbling in these areas at Reed, I took a year off and spent it at California State University at Northridge taking accounting and business classes. I was surprised to soon find my interest growing in these areas, as they seemed more in step with real world matters than my course work at Reed.

After completing the year at CSUN, I returned to complete my final two years at Reed—although I knew I would pursue Accounting and Business after graduation (and probably one of the few "Reedies" to ever go into this line of work!). I could have transferred to CSUN, but I still wanted the best education I felt I could get. Even if my Reed Economics degree wasn't going to do anything specifically for me, I felt more complete and educated having earned it. Besides, I would have hated to quit!

After my Reed undergraduate experiences were complete, I spent one more year finishing up my Accounting courses at CSUN. I was ready to enter the world of Public Accounting. From the beginning I knew that this field was a bridge to my MBA, and that as soon as I spent a few years earning my CPA, I would attend business school in preparation for my long term career in finance. I found Public Accounting a difficult, grueling life, although one that prepares you extremely well for the challenges ahead. Think of it as boot camp for Accountants. After two years in this profession, I was a CPA. I soon applied to and was accepted to UCLA's MBA Program, and started the next fall.

When I entered the MBA Program, I wasn't sure what direction I wanted my career to take, other than the fact that it would be in finance. When a finance-oriented individual enters a MBA Program, there are typically a few standard options. The areas of Consulting/Investment Banking/Trading is certainly one of the most popular paths. Companies actually come to campus, and search you out. For the more traditional "Corporation Finance" (i.e. working for a company in a finance related capacity), only a handful of companies come to school.

At that point knowing only what I didn't want to do, I took as many finance courses as I could. Nothing was very industry specific, and therefore not very helpful in terms of career selection. The first summer was approaching, so I began to search the Job Placement Office for potential internships. I ended up receiving a job offer for the summer working for Summit Health, a health care company that owned a number of hospitals and nursing facilities.

The position as a Financial Analyst was appealing, and so I accepted and spent the next seven months (extending part time into the school year) working with the Director of Finance on a whole series of special projects and strategic analyses. One project was a determination of whether we should keep or sell a mail order pharmaceutical company; another, the cost/benefit analyses for different departments within our various hospitals.

With this experience under my belt, I was very interested in remaining in the health care industry. But as I began to finish out my last year of UCLA, I was unable to find any health care companies that actually were looking for MBAs on campus. With the support of our Career Placement

Center, I ended up networking with a number of individuals who were already in Health Care, and began approaching a number of health care companies. One of these individuals at Blue Cross of California referred me to a Finance Manager in one of the divisions. I received a call requesting an interview—a few interviews later I was employed in health care.

I had assumed that my MBA would be a major factor both in terms of obtaining a position and enhancing my future career path. I was a bit surprised—and taken aback—that for companies that don't specifically go out of their way to hire MBAs, that having such a background—even from a good school—won't necessarily be a huge factor. Your MBA may be an excellent way to network, it may get you in the door if you can get your resume to another AGSM (Anderson) graduate, but don't expect the organization to necessarily pay a great deal of attention to the degree. Further, as you begin to work for a period of years, your MBA background may be forgotten. I think that much of this is due to the fact that by far and away the preferred background of choice from the Finance Department side is a CPA background—Big 6 being the most coveted. In many finance organizations, a MBA background seems to have limited value.

When I first started working for BCC, my role was as a Financial Analyst for a division selling Group Insurance to the 51+market. It was a very interesting time to join BCC. A new management team had come on board a few years earlier and were now enacting dramatic organizational changes. Although at this point I was a CPA, this position didn't draw much upon that knowledge. Rather it revolved mostly around budgeting and analysis. Our unit was divided into different segments—one budgeting, one actual performance. By my placement in the budgeting unit, I was not able to draw much upon my accounting experiences. Had I been involved in the other segment of the department, I would have drawn on my CPA skills, but at the expense of learning the budgeting and analysis facets of finance.

After a few years of budgeting and analysis as an analyst and later as a Supervisor of Financial Analysis, I was promoted to a Manager of

Finance in another division. This position came with a staff of about six, and was a much more challenging position. I was responsible for a series of businesses, while at the same time, spending virtually all my time with my company's recapitalization (the non-profit company converted to for-profit). Although I enjoyed working with my boss (a Director of Finance), my time was so taxed by the two competing duties above, that I began to work long hours trying just to keep up. I was in part an inexperienced manager, and inefficient in terms of using my resources (analysts) and in part was trying to juggle two separate full-time jobs. Although I was working extremely hard, I was learning a great deal and enjoyed my colleagues at work. As soon as the recap was completed successfully, my division was dissolved and I was assigned to a unit that was never in my long term plans. I was able to quickly land a Finance Manager position in another division within Blue Cross. This position has since become one of the best work experiences I have had.

This division sells managed care products in states other than California. My particular unit sells insurance to individuals, small groups (3-50 employees), standard business (51-250 employees), and seniors. Since the unit was a start-up, no funds were available for staff. I started the unit completely from scratch. As a division just being formed, in the middle of numerous system conversions, we had been forced to start virtually everything from the beginning. None of the work was set up for us, and it has been a tremendous experience to learn everything from ground zero. As the top financial individual in this particular segment of our division, I have a great deal of latitude as to how I want to approach things or who I want to hire or how I wish to organize the department. As my department handles all the affairs of our division, we are exposed to all areas of Accounting and Finance, work on interesting analyses, work with Actuaries on pricing, and continually interact with the general managers and other senior officers. I am finally getting an excellent opportunity to utilize managerial skills as well as those that I learned in public accounting.

What exactly does a Finance Manager do? In my current capacity, the following are many of my specific duties:

* ## Responsibility for the Monthly Accounting Close and Financial Analysis

Are the Administrative Expenses properly recorded? Are they classified to the correct areas? Are they reasonable, or are they out of line? Are the Profit and Loss Statements correct? Why are there increases/decreases from the prior month? Is there a variance to the Annual Budget? Why? Will it continue? In my unit, we perform all accounting as well as finance functions; in some larger companies or divisions, depending on how they are structured, these functions may be split into separate units. Financial analysis and variance analysis are functions typically performed by all Finance Managers. These and many other issues lie at the heart of any finance manager's responsibilities. I am constantly asked about our unit's performance, and make monthly presentations to the company's Controller. We will receive occasional questions directly from the President of our division as well. A Finance Manager is the one person fully responsible for making sure that the appropriate accounting entries are made, that they are properly reflected in the Financial Reporting Systems, and that we can explain all variances and understand exactly what is happening. This type of work may be somewhat anxiety producing (especially when large variances first come up!), but is also interesting in that you have a hand in the financial results for your area. The way I've organized my unit is to have one Financial Analyst dedicated to each business—anything that happens in that business is their responsibility. By doing this, the Finance Manager can pull out of the day to day mechanics and more fully see the big picture and direct activities as appropriate.

* Responsibility for Budgeting

I wish I could say this is one of my favorite duties, but it isn't! (Perhaps because I've done it so long). Most organizations spend a great deal of time budgeting their future administrative expenses, then set targets for future profit objectives needed to meet their organizational goals. This usually involves a 3 or 5 year plan, and a more detailed annual plan. Once completed, this is the benchmark that actuals are compared to for the rest of the year. In addition, many organizations (especially publicly owned entities) will also reforecast quarterly during the year. Forecasting is beneficial for a unit in that it forces you to plan all possible contingencies, and gets an organization thinking in the right direction—critically on how to improve results. The better the plans, the better the understanding of the actual results that follow. When this is accomplished, a company is in a better position to make changes beneficial to their future. The negative side to this is that the work is very detailed, and sometimes can involve many deadlines and time pressures. A good knowledge of this is essential for a successful career in Finance.

* Special Projects

This will take the rest of your time up, and will often be the most interesting—and complex—part of your job. System conversions that don't fully work, and book incorrect information or incomplete information to the G/L. New definitions or conversions in businesses—perhaps a new State that your company is doing business in—is not being picked up correctly in the general ledger or other financial systems. Estimates of what would happen if a unit was dissolved and merged into another. Transfer of business from one unit to another. Information requests from auditors and outside agencies. Special deals cut with different outside agencies to sell your product, and the determination of how to administer them.

Special calls from high level personnel wanting information prepared for them immediately. Various profitability analyses for new products, new regions, or new entities.

* Responsibility for Hiring and Maintaining an Organization

What I consider the most important responsibility for a manager is attracting and maintaining the personnel in the department. Although all organizations differ, and a manager may have significant powers to hire and organize or relatively little, this will most likely determine a manager's success. Not only should the manager not be personally involved in each issue that comes up (it will detract from the bigger picture) but a manager will not be able to do everything that needs to be done. To me, this is the biggest pitfall that can occur, but the easiest one to fall into. There is a great comfort in knowing each and every detail, but by staying in this comfort zone, it will invariably take you away from the work that you really need to do to be successful. If you are a manager, manage—don't do! Simple words, but ones that are very difficult to work towards. The only way to get there is by building up staff that you trust, and empowering them.

In conclusion, here are a number of recommendations that I would make for those considering Health Care from the Payer side in the Finance capacity:

Depending on the firm, expect that your MBA's importance may not be quite what you would want it to be. Its impact may range from being helpful to being only somewhat relevant.

Finance anywhere is a very detailed, sometimes grueling profession. It will probably more often than you expect come down to mechanics and details, although this is not to say that the big picture isn't extremely critical as well.

There are a great deal of time pressures related to this line of work. Although some of your projects will take place over a specific period of time, don't be surprised to have lots of 'emergencies'. For some, emergencies are only somewhat palatable, and they figure that if they only plan ahead better, most can be eliminated. These individuals soon learn that as important as planning ahead is, much of this is unavoidable, and it is important to be flexible as well as to not overreact to the pressures, and to be able to stomach them as a required facet of your job.

A CPA, preferably from a large Public Accounting firm, is very important to success in finance. Without a CPA, you run a large risk of being displaced by newer Big 6 CPAs when management changes are made. This is not to say that it can't be done, but you may face a large obstacle.

If you are what you eat, then you are what you hire. Give in and hire "pretty good" people, and your units performance will never be all that good. Hold out, use temps if necessary, but hire wisely!

When you stop learning, it is time to move on to another position—a larger company allows you to move around into different positions without leaving entirely.

Associate Hospital Chief of Staff

David Auerbach, MD, MBA

Physician colleagues often ask me about the advisability of pursuing an MBA degree. My answer is that it depends entirely on one's career plans. I do not believe that the time and expense of an MBA are necessarily justified for someone who intends to manage a small practice, become a division chief or chair at an academic health center, or even hold office as chief of staff at a medical center. On the other hand, if the physician's aspirations include a position where business acumen is as important as clinical judgment, particularly where the responsibility is organization-wide and includes financial accountability, the MBA is likely to be a good investment.

For those who chose not to obtain an MBA, I offer as an alternative my "one sentence MBA": Organizations that have a single mission do better than those with multiple missions; those which are tightly organized do better than those which are loosely organized. That's it. The observation may sound simple, but as far as I can tell, it was a primary or secondary theme of most of the hundreds of case studies I read in my Executive MBA Program.

This is not to say that you should take this insight so literally as to avoid challenges. In fact, I have spent most of my career at academic health centers, perhaps the most egregious example of a multiple mission, loosely organized institution. More on that later.

As I think about the experiences that have shaped my thinking as a manager, they seem to fall into four categories: my clinical and epidemiological experience; learning to be a primary care internist "provider" in the burgeoning managed care environment of Southern California in the 1980s and early 1990s; my MBA training; and shopping at a Nordstrom department store.

Clinical and Epidemiological Experience

My training and experience as an internist is the foundation of my development as a physician executive. There were many lessons learned, starting with a recognition of what an extraordinary challenge it is to efficiently manage patient care processes. Health care must be the most complex of all service industries. To frame this point in the dry language of economics, in what other industry could you generate a serious debate about whether a good "outcome" (e.g., a healthy patient) is the result of good service quality or the result of "raw material" (e.g., patient) selection? Providing a quality service as critical and personal as health care to a group as diverse as the individuals who populate the typical waiting room or surgical suite may be the managerial equivalent of climbing Mount Everest. Even the seemingly simple act of explaining a treatment plan must be customized for the needs of the barely literate and the Nobel laureate; I have personally cared for both.

Early in the process of acculturation to the world of care providers, the characteristics needed to survive and flourish become clear. A medical school professor once assured us that, where we were going, thoroughness was more important than intelligence. This proved an accurate assessment. Attention to detail is the key. Initially, the focus is on the details of the patient's condition. Then, typically, attention shifts to the details associated with making sure the patient will be able to navigate those complex systems we have devised to care for her. Trying to improve those systems has become one of my main professional assignments.

On the other hand, some of the talents needed to be a good manager are conspicuously absent from clinical education. One is the need to prioritize and manage time. For a medical intern, long-range planning largely consists of answering the question "What do I need to do so that I can eventually go home tonight?" Even as a practitioner, the focus is on the patient in front of you at the moment. As a manger, the need to consider a more distant time horizon, measured in months and years, becomes crucial. There is never enough time, never adequate resources. Prioritization is mandatory.

Lifting my gaze above the patient in front of me, and beyond the current day, became a habit during my two post-residency years as a medical epidemiologist for the Centers for Disease Control (CDC). The epidemiologist looks at populations and trends over time, often very long periods of time. The issue is not how to treat the patient of the moment, but what policies will promote public health. Epidemiological experience turned out to be fortuitous leavening for a clinician en route to becoming a physician executive. The experience was further enriched by the location and timing of my CDC experience. I was sent to Los Angeles just two months after the first cases of a new disease were reported. This disease came to be known as AIDS. I participated in the first national case control study on AIDS and was responsible for the field work that identified the first transfusion-related case of AIDS. I also found myself near the center of the public policy, political and media crisis that surrounded the AIDS epidemic.

Managed Care

As an internist in southern California in the mid-1980s, I learned to be characterized by a whole new set of euphemisms: "PCP" (primary care physician), "provider", and, most disparagingly, "gatekeeper." Managed care had arrived, and I received a practical education in the new world of health care financing. I was fortunate to be educated in the company of a superb group of internists at a large academic health center. A single capitated, full-risk bearing HMO contract rapidly grew to nearly half of our clinical business. We learned the importance of managing utilization and coordinating care. At a weekly meeting of the entire group, we prospectively approved all non-emergency referrals to specialists and reviewed all emergency room visits and hospitalizations. Over time, the routine practices of a diverse group of internists converged on a more consistent pattern of patient management. Once these mechanisms were firmly established, the program became a gratifying win-win-win situation: our patients received excellent care (in some ways better than our non-HMO patients because of the explicit obligation to coordinate care optimally); the HMO was pleased with our performance; and, once managed properly, these capitated patients became financially advantageous for our group. In short, the lesson is that success is predictable when organizational incentives are tightly aligned.

Business School

Actually, I was pleased to attend a school with the more appealing designation of Graduate School of Management. The first year seemed devoted to filling in, at least partly, large gaps in my management knowledge, particularly in the areas of finance and economics. The focus of the second year was to synthesize and apply concepts learned earlier. At the orientation session at the beginning of our first year, one of the speakers mentioned that in an Executive MBA program, we were likely to learn as much from our classmates as from our professors. That was an accurate prediction. The class consisted of very intelligent and energetic mid to upper level managers, mostly at large corporations. We challenged and learned from each other both in class and perhaps even more in our study groups.

With only one other physician in my class of 60, health care was rarely an explicit topic of discussion, and even then only mentioned as cost of doing business that reduces profitability. However, the concepts that were developed were nearly always applicable to health care organizations. For example, one of the great lessons of microeconomics, the concept of economies of scale, is as germane to health care as it is in any other setting. Equally pertinent is one of the key concepts of organizational behavior, that of dis-economies of large scale. The latter may become especially relevant as consolidation in health care continues, and we face the daunting challenge of offering a highly personal service by very large organizations. This is just the kind of management paradox that Professor Ouchi relished.

I was often struck by the difference in personality between my management school classmates and most of my medical school classmates from years earlier. My business school colleagues appeared to have greater tolerance for risk. If you told one of them that his industry was about to experience major upheaval, and that the market would put enormous pressure on profitability, his next thought might be "That surely is bad news for someone; but I'm going to figure out how to profit from this change." Presented with the same circumstance, many physicians are more likely to go through the stages of someone diagnosed with a terminal illness, as characterized by Elizabeth Kubler-Ross in On Death and Dying (denial, anger, bargaining, depression, and, finally, acceptance). Among the attractions of a medical career in my generation was that it was something of a sure bet; one could hardly be unsuccessful, at least financially. Those who gravitated to business sought no such guarantee. Yet, in the new world of managed care, learning to live with risk is crucial. Helping colleagues appreciate this may be the most important contribution to a health care organization that can be made by an MD/MBA.

Shopping at Nordstrom

Nordstrom is the extraordinarily successful Seattle-based department store chain, with an emphasis on selling clothes and other fashion items. While I know nothing about the retail business, and do not like to shop for clothes, the secret of Nordstrom's success became immediately clear when I moved to the west coast and walked into the store for the first time: the sales staff is single-mindedly devoted to customer service. The customer loyalty generated by this attitude results in profitability that far exceeds their competitors. If the reason for this profitability is so obvious, then why don't these competitors emulate the Nordstrom approach? The answer, apparently, is that it is not easy to hire, train, and motivate staff to this level of customer focus.

This lesson is central to my notion of what management is all about: hiring the best people, then motivating them to do their best work. Sure, having good data, and making astute decisions, is important. But in a service industry, nothing is more important than having the best people at all levels of the organization.

Conclusion

As health care moves from a cottage industry to a highly centralized, corporate mode of organization, opportunities for physician executives will continue to grow. I have had the opportunity to grow professionally in the setting of a large, academic health center, first in California and then in Florida. The multiple missions of patient care, teaching and research are exciting and challenging. While I have learned a great deal on the job the past few years, so has the academic health center. The lesson of the "one sentence MBA" applies: the way to compensate for having multiple missions is to be more tightly organized, not less.

Consultant

Greg Vigen, MBA, FSA

Through an MBA degree, actuarial exams, and lots of effort, I have been fortunate to have an exciting and productive career. I work for a major employee benefit firm as a principal focusing on financial management of health care.

This is a great time to be in the health care industry and the industry needs a lot of management expertise. This will give a brief summary of the opportunities in the industry, some personal background, then discuss some of my experiences which may be helpful to others thinking of the field.

Healthcare Industry

The health industry is probably the most dynamic industry in the country. The historical cottage industry is being transformed to a business environment. These changes are putting substantial pressures on cost without clear definitions of quality.

This is driven by economics. Statistics indicate a vast oversupply of hospitals and some specialties of physicians across the country. Hospitals in some locations are operating at close to marginal costs. Physicians are seeing extensive pressure on compensation and working more frequently in multi-physician settings, instead of solo practice.

Companies which used to provide unlimited funds for their employees, are now becoming more active managers. Providers and carriers are under pressure to organize and modify their systems. Also, the dynamics of the industry vary greatly from one location to another. This is creating tremendous opportunities and challenges.

This magnitude of change really levels the playing field. Experience in the industry is sometimes a detriment, as old paradigms become obsolete. The health industry did not historically attracted as many talented managers as other industries, so talented people move quickly within their organizations.

The combined impact of this is a tremendous need for managerial, financial, and clinical staff.

Personal Background

My undergraduate degree was in mathematics, with course work in computers and business. This financial and computer background continue to be my strengths. After looking over various jobs during my senior year, I opted to start an MBA program directly after undergraduate work. Although this might not work for everyone, I had worked at several seasonal jobs which provided me with a business perspective.

While working on my MBA, I passed the first three tests in a series of professional exams. These "actuarial exams" are sponsored by the insurance industry and are similar in concept to those for the accounting and legal professions. These tests provided an extensive background in the pension and health care industry. Eventually, I completed the full series of tests for a designation of FSA (Fellow of the Society of Actuaries).

In addition to the technical knowledge described above, my other key business characteristics are:
- A strong work ethic with continuing focus on solutions
- Strategic thinking with an analytic perspective
- Building on my strengths (especially early in my career)
- Teaming with others who counterbalance my weaknesses

Deborah Shlian, MD, MBA and Clint Patterson, PhD, MBA

Many MBAs have different skills and styles than I have. Others may excel in relationships, organization, sales, or in other areas. Many have less focus on technical skills. The key for each individual is to develop the right blend for their ability and style. My sense, from watching many successful people in many organizations is that clear strengths offset several moderate weaknesses until you reach senior management levels.

Guiding Concepts: Early Career

The core concepts come in three major categories: technical knowledge and skills, breadth of business sense, and choice of industry and job.

In terms of technical knowledge and skills, understanding computers, business, communications is essential in today's health care environment. Although all three of these were available from the MBA program, I spent most of my college effort on the first two. This forced me to spend a lot of effort to improve my communication skills after graduation. For example, I could never write fast enough and legibly enough to keep up with my thoughts. Fortunately, I am now a moderately good typist which has made quite an improvement in my written communications and formal presentations.

The combination of the MBA and actuarial exams provides me with a unique set of skills in the industry. There are few people who both understand the insurance industry and management. Application of this technical knowledge makes me relatively distinct.

These skills become more critical as the medical system changes. Providers are no longer being paid on an indemnity basis (for each visit or test) but must take broader responsibility for delivering health care to a population. Management must communicate with a range of players, the business and financial elements must coordinate, and systems must be in place to support these efforts.

Analytic work is as much art as science. Historical financial data is indemnity based, but does not reflect the new system. The behavior changes rapidly as providers understand the new requirements and new reward systems are implemented. Also, few controls on underutilization of services are in place.

Business Sense

The health care industry is changing extraordinarily rapidly. The ability to identify alternatives and use good business judgment to prioritize and organize the options is critical. An MBA mindset of viewing the system at its broadest level is critical. Although the "best" alternative is not always clear, my experience from my MBA let me avoid the "worst" alternatives. In addition the various MBA tools, ranging from systems analysis, financial analysis, presentation skills, leading meetings, are quite valuable.

Strategic Choice of Industry and Job

The business sense discussed above played a vital role in my choice of industry and job. When I graduated from UCLA, I did not take a standard MBA route. I looked at several different industries before taking a job at an insurance company in health care. The decision was based on three key thoughts: health insurance and employee benefits was a growing industry, the company provided a good place to learn, and my competition was limited (few MBAs or talented staff were working in this industry).

Currently, health care management is probably even a clearer choice than it was years ago when I made my decision. It is an industry undergoing rapid change with far less staff resources than it needs. It is an easy place to have a quick impact.

While the choice of industry is clear, it is less clear what company to chose and which job to take. Substantial investments are needed to be a major force in the market. The potential jumbo employers, consulting firms, hospitals, physician groups, insurance carriers, and HMOs, are all fighting for either major growth, or, in some cases, their existence. In addition, although Wall Street focuses on the jumbo, publicly traded companies, as potential employers there are a number of smaller firms with strong market niches.

Each player is going through change. Many consulting firms have merged, or have widely varying strengths. Similarly, hospitals are closing or merging, and physicians are forming organized groups. In the last five years, all but three of the top ten health insurance carriers have sold their businesses. For the most part, regional HMOs have taken their places.

Guiding Concepts: Later Career

Possibly the most important concepts are flexibility (and welcoming change), transitioning from doing to managing, eliminating weaknesses, and providing clear value.

Flexibility—During the middle of my career, there were several key times when my direction had to change. While the specific problems are much different today, good career planning means you need to both anticipate challenges in advance and take action to do things differently. Given the volatility of the health care market, it is critical to know how and when to change direction.

The first time I had to make a major change was in the late 1970s, several years after graduation. It became clear that:

- The computer systems were very weak
- Basic financial information was unavailable
- The major players had no commitment to change

Because of these challenges, I left from health operations, and moved to the pension side of employee benefits. It took several years for the industry dynamics to improve. At that point, I moved back to the health insurance operation.

Even though lots of time has passed, these dynamics are still critical. Systems and financial information are still critical topics. In addition, there is still a lot of resistance to change. Those organizations still concerned about the past and are not enthusiastic about change are likely to be gone in the next few years.

My second major change occurred when I recognized that the company was ready to leave the business. The parent company was very frustrated with the health care subsidiary for which I worked. The signs were fairly clear to an MBA; the company was making the company attractive enough to get a good sales price.

Since I had now learned much of what I needed, I started an interview process that led me to move to a consulting firm. That firm, William Mercer, is the one I'm working for now.

Transition from doer to manager

Most employees, and many people working in the healthcare industry, are rewarded for getting things done. For example, doctors and nurses are paid to see patients. This set of skills and style needed to be successful in most jobs is quite different from what a manager needs. The new skills, and the willingness to discard old skills has been a major blockage in some people's career. The new skills, such as working through others, and keeping a broad perspective of the organization and mission, often contradict the skills that first make one successful.

Personally, balancing these skills is still a battle. Although others have had much more problems with this. I have seen many talented people who have stopped at a middle career level primarily because of this inability to transition. This comes in many forms. For example, one very talented recruit, ended up going back to school, thinking that he needed more technical knowledge, when the problem was that they actually got stuck in the details far too often.

Eliminating Weaknesses

Through middle management and even at senior levels in some organizations, being very strong in one or two areas creates a very successful career. However, at some point future career growth requires you to minimize or eliminate some weaknesses.

I've already discussed the changes in my communications skills over the years. A current personal challenge is in the area of implementation. I am a troubleshooter by nature. Once a solid solution is identified, my instinct is to move on to something new. This has generally worked quite well in consulting assignments historically, but the industry now is looking for both strategy and implementation. Rather than get left behind, I have to adapt my role to meet the new demands.

Clear Value

In the long term, the one common denominator between all the successful business people is providing value and making sure your contributions are clear. The opportunity for valuable work is here. Although there are many talented people in the industry, given the fact that 17% of the economy is devoted to healthcare, many more are needed. On the other hand, the challenges are just as large. Creating an organized, cost-effective medical system while improving the quality is a huge undertaking.

Some of you may have seen an old Chinese curse (or blessing, depending on how you take it). "May you live in interesting times".

The times are surely interesting in the health care industry. It's up to us to turn this into a blessing and make this into a system that we can take proud in.

Entrepreneur

Richard Eidinger, MD, MBA

In Search of the Steepest Path

For as long as I can remember I've been interested in business. My family was a medical family in a socialist country and so I did the only thing a non-hockey playing capitalist kid could do–I became a doctor. Canadians have a tremendous pride in their health care system and the social net that provides cradle to grave benefits to all. However the society is suspicious of successful business people who somehow manage to shrug off the national culture of mediocrity and assemble more than their "fair" share. For a time the country put their physicians squarely in their economic blind spot and allowed them to have societal prestige and a double helping at the table of socialism. Devoid of a family business to run and in an era that preceded the rise of the MBA, medicine seemed a decent choice. I began the program and found the study of Internal Medicine very interesting. However, as my training proceeded, I increasingly became aware of the relentless, emotionally draining, piecework that is the nature of medical practice.

In 1985 my parents decided that they had had enough of the balmy weather in Saskatchewan and opted to move to Seattle. My father began a practice of Allergy and Immunology, which fortunately quickly prospered. As I finished my training in medicine, I decided that it was time for a change and I took advantage of US immigration laws that allowed me to immigrate as a permanent resident. I had decided on the medical subspecialty of gastroenterology. It was a very interesting area within medicine with lots of exciting procedures. I looked at a number of programs and was fortunate to be selected by the program at UCLA. In August 1987 I arrived on a nonstop flight from Toronto to Los Angeles to begin my fellowship at UCLA and a new life in a new country.

It was quickly apparent that I wasn't in Canada anymore. There were miles of shops, miles of cars; the air was electric with the fervor of millions of my fellow Los Angelinos working at getting ahead. Over the first few months of my residency, I began to moonlight as an Internist at both for-profit and not-for-profit hospitals. The practice was very different from what I had known. There were bills, slips, and charges for everything. This new thing sweeping California called managed care concerned the doctors. Most impressive was the unbelievable size of health care as a business. I had gone from a nationalized instrument of government policy to a bit player in a health care monolith. For a time I wasn't sure what to make of it, however as with most things in life there seemed to be winners and losers. I felt that I couldn't simply allow myself to be carried along in what was clearly becoming a very turbulent market.

In 1988, I met a neighbor in my apartment building who turned out to be the critical influence at a significant time in my life. Dave had graduated from the Graduate School of Management (GSM) at UCLA in the late 70's. He had been a management consultant in the Middle East and was now back in LA seeking his fortune.

Dave and I became fast friends as we talked about the possibilities in health care. We decided that we would try and purchase a medical supply company. The plan was that I would go in as the doctor guy and get my "brothers and sisters" to buy sutures and Dave would run the business. As I watched Dave analyze the opportunity, I saw discipline and process. He approached the opportunity the same way that I approached physical diagnosis. Unfortunately the venture didn't succeed, but I had been privy to a process that provided critical insight. If I was going to be a businessperson

I needed to learn the skills of business. In the summer of 1988 I decided I would leave medicine and begin the full time study of management as soon as possible.

In September, 1989 I arrived at The Anderson School to begin my studies. My class was an extraordinary tapestry of personalities, talents and nationalities. I had never had the American College experience so the closest I had been to ivy of any sort was a childhood stint at camp. Over the next two years I tried to balance part-time medical practice (read: bill paying) with the demands of the full-time program. The period was a critical formative stage during which the physician mindset began to be molded by the discipline of management. Though the AGSM years were my 12th and 13th postgraduate years and I was, in general, tired of school, I enjoyed them far more than anything else I had ever studied.

During the summer of 1990, I was selected to participate in the Venture Capital Fellows Program at AGSM. I got a summer position with Peregrine Ventures and worked under the supervision of Gene Miller. It was the first time that I had a chance to see the venture capital model. I was introduced to companies that were jammed with human capital and then given the money to execute against the hopes and dreams of a management team and their investors. I learned about deal control, worked financial statements and bore witness to failure in business. The experience of that summer fundamentally changed my aspirations as a businessperson. I decided during that summer that one day I would have my breakthrough idea, my management team, my venture financing and that together we would take on the market and create value where none had existed before. To this day I believe that the well executed venture model, for those who earn the right to participate, is the pinnacle of business achievement.

The Anderson years provided two more exceedingly important experiences. I had the opportunity to take James Q. Wilson's course titled the Morality of Capitalism. The class was a showcase for Wilson's belief that economics drive most of human behavior. More impressive from my standpoint was his view that the fruits of capitalism, among other things wealth creation, had to a significant degree bought and paid for much of the democratic freedom we now enjoy. He encouraged us to appreciate that superior performance in business should be regarded as a high calling. At around this time, I became eligible for US citizenship. I took my oath of citizenship with thousands of others most of whom had struggled far more than I for the prize of becoming a naturalized American. It is difficult for those that are native born to appreciate the impact that becoming a citizen has. The mix of these events solidified my personal philosophy to wage business in order to return to other stakeholders and myself the greatest success the market and our skills would allow.

In 1991, I was graduated from the Anderson School and went to work for a managed care company called FHP, Inc. Robert Gumbiner, a physician, entrepreneur and health care visionary started the company in the 1960s. Though FHP had faults, it had many strengths as well and was an ideal place for a newly minted "physician executive" (as we then began to be called) to learn the business of health care. FHP had a very strong, almost military culture. We were cost focussed, disciplined, organized, and determined that FHP should succeed as rapidly as the opportunity for our products allowed. The company culture was so strong that years after working at FHP, company alumni meet and spontaneously reminisce about FHP's heyday. In addition to the positives, I also had a chance to come to understand that a prevailing attitude existed among non-physician health care managers that doctors just weren't good business managers. It was clear to me that a glass ceiling existed separating me from a general management role with profit and loss responsibility. If I was going to get my venture backed company, I needed to demonstrate the ability to create value for shareholders.

In 1994, I was offered a bridge to general management within Aetna Health Plans and accepted it without hesitation. I worked for Aetna in California and Arizona. In the spring of 1995, I moved to Phoenix to become the Chief Executive Officer of Aetna's Health Plan in Arizona (AHPA). It was an extraordinarily valuable experience at an ideal time.

Aetna had been progressively decentralizing functions into the field and as a result there was an opportunity to build a team, make a plan and execute against it. AHPA grew rapidly, innovated relentlessly, and quickly was regarded as having one of the best management teams of any of the Aetna Plans. Unfortunately the centralized style of the Plan's new owners caused the sun to set on some of the most exciting and innovative days that Aetna had seen in Arizona. Nonetheless, the two years that I spent with Aetna were invaluable for me, for our employees and for our shareholders.

As I write this, I have spent the last year working towards the goal I set in the summer of 1990 and have worked at since. I am the President & CEO of a small specialty health care insurance company called ACTIVA HealthGroup, Inc. in Phoenix. I came into the Company with one of my closest friends, a business kindred spirit, who is also a classmate from Anderson. We are locked in a raw battle to create a sustainable business model in our niche and clearly define the value that we believe is available for harvest. We have received expressions of interest from some of the Silicon Valley's leading venture capital funds. The experience uses few of my corporate skills; I haven't worn a suit in a year. The battle for ACTIVA is a highly personal struggle that is fought at a gut level with each and every gyration of our nascent business. It requires my partner and I to focus and execute and focus and execute, over and over again. Our journey up this steepest of paths may at some point lead to personal wealth but it has already lead to great self-knowledge. It is the essence of business and for those with the requisite courage, I highly recommend it.

INFORMATION SYSTEMS EXECUTIVE

Mike Wall, MBA

The health care information systems arena is undergoing significant change, as hospitals, physician groups, and insurance companies require more clinically-based, patient-centered systems to manage care. When asked to describe my career in healthcare management, I had an opportunity to reflect on my career aspirations and key decisions, and to identify some the challenges I faced, as a manager in a rapidly changing industry.

Where do I start? What should I write that would be valuable to MBA students? I will start at the place I am now. I am currently the Vice President, Information Services, for Accountable Oncology Associates (AOA), a cancer disease management firm. Working on behalf of HMOs and other risk bearing entities, AOA manages the multiple specialists and providers involved in cancer care. I am responsible for developing and overseeing AOA's information technology strategy. This includes leading a team of data analysts and programmers who design and support the clinical and claims information systems necessary to manage cancer care providers. Superior information services enable us to understand and then reduce costs, without sacrificing clinical quality or patient satisfaction.

Background: Childhood to College

The road to my current position began as early as my childhood, when my mother used to say I had the hands to be a good physician. Growing up in a family where my three uncles were physicians, I was exposed to both the clinical and business sides of health care. I went to Dartmouth College in 1976, planning to master the pre-med science courses as well as benefit from a liberal arts education. I was not alone, as over 50% of my entering freshman class also figured medicine would be a respected, secure, and financially rewarding career. Needless to say, several of us would eventually refine our interests. Some of us figured it out in college. One of my classmates went so far as to complete an Internal Medicine residency before opting for an MBA and a career in venture capital.

For me, mediocre performances in organic chemistry and genetics encouraged me to shift gears into other courses of study. I excelled in political science courses and had the great opportunity to take a health economics course from Jack Wennberg, MD, MPH. Dr. Wennberg eventually became famous for his "small area practice pattern variation" studies, which showed higher surgical rates per capita, in areas where there were higher numbers of surgeons. This course inspired my interest in health care management and policy issues.

I gained a real world perspective on the health care industry during college, when I served as an administrative intern at a major urban hospital in California. While working for the director of planning, I discovered that hospital administrators were concerned with more than surgical supplies and nursing hours. They were involved in complex relationships with medical staff, trustees, patients, press, legislators, and the community. In this internship, I helped organize a statewide planning conference entitled "Health: Whose Responsibility?" I gained much insight from the conference's dialogues between a nurse and medical educator, between the director of the $4 billion a year Medi-Cal program (1979 estimate) and the governor (then Jerry Brown), between a holistic teacher and a physician. I began to unravel for myself the assumptions, traditions, and values that underlie our perceptions of healers and health care institutions.

From College to the Real World

In my senior year of college, I wrote the following in my application to the Johns Hopkins School of Public Health. "Further study at a school of public health seems essential to deepening my theoretical understanding of the issues and equipping myself with the proper analytical tools. I also hope to complement my MPH with an MBA or doctorate in the administrative sciences. Once I fully understand the present institutions, I want to move on to a new agenda of carefully planned and credentialized forms of health care delivery such as hospices, satellite clinics, and HMOs where the thrust of these programs is health promotion, not health dependence. Like our world energy supply, health care is a resource that is wasted, maldistributed, costly, and scarce. Too many people are dissatisfied with the impersonality and inadequacy of care. With the proper training and experience, I hope to become a sensitive mediator between providers and consumers of health care."

It was interesting to go back 17 years and read what I had said about my career ideals and aspirations. I found it reassuring that I have stuck to some of my original beliefs, although not all my intentions.

I decided to forego my acceptance to Johns Hopkins. I felt that the MPH degree was a "soft degree." I was more interested in gaining some business experience and later, applying to business school.

My first job out of college was with the management consulting services department of a then Big Eight accounting firm, Deloitte Haskins & Sells (now Deloitte and Touche). At Deloitte during the early eighties, most of the consulting work involved systems planning for audit clients. My first assignment was a "systems design project" for a Veterans Administration retirement home. My health care systems career was launched!

I look back on that first job and recognize that technical expertise was important, yet not nearly as essential as understanding a client's needs and translating those requirements for system vendors and programmers. I found I could never know everything about bits and bytes, and the latest in software and hardware. Yet as long as I constantly asked good questions of both the users and the vendors, performed in depth analysis, and developed strategic and tactical plans to meet their needs, I would be successful in health care systems.

The health care industry has historically lagged other industries in the use of information systems technology. Therefore, thinking about and deploying proven applications from other industries like financial services has also proved worthwhile to my career development.

I learned another key lesson from my first job as a consultant in a Big Eight accounting firm. Specifically, I developed a financial orientation to problem solving. By paying attention to what others called details such as the latest in Medicare reimbursement regulations or the balance sheet of a systems vendor or the cash flow of a rapidly growing, multi-unit provider, I found myself in a stronger position to assist clients with financially sound advice on complicated issues.

After three years at Deloitte, I moved on to a position as an associate in the health care consulting practice of Booz Allen & Hamilton. There I capitalized on my financial skills and industry expertise to perform successfully in a role normally reserved for those with an MBA or MPH. I worked on a variety of strategic planning projects for multi-hospital systems and insurance companies. Both the HMO and the personal computer industries were rapidly developing in 1983. My assignments at Booz Allen required that I think about the impact of these technology and health care trends, such as: paperless claims processing systems, hospitals diversifying into related areas such as home health, and insurance companies setting up HMO subsidiaries. This was long before the term "managed care" was even in vogue. At Booz Allen, I was privileged to work in the company of thought leaders in both health care and technology. This consulting environment was humbling and challenging. It was fast-paced and required constant travel and long hours. I established contacts and skill sets that have helped me several times over in subsequent positions.

UCLA Business School Experience

After five years of health care consulting, I decided it was an opportune time to go to business school. I wanted to refine my technical skills and concentrate on the knowledge that would enable me to take on management responsibilities.

In 1985, I enrolled in UCLA's MBA program. In addition to acquiring the specific knowledge of corporate finance and product marketing, I wanted to learn about different business opportunities and career paths. At this time in the mid-eighties, the Wall Street firms were anxious to recruit UCLA MBA students because of the school's outstanding reputation in finance. I was a likely candidate for these firms, due to my financial and consulting experience.

However, I was equally intrigued with startup companies and a more entrepreneurial career. For one of UCLA's courses in Entrepreneurial Studies, I wrote a business plan to use computer aided design and manufacturing (CAD/CAM) to make artificial limbs. We ended up winning the top prize in UCLA's annual venture capital competition.

By the spring of my first year, I had a summer internship offer to go to the First Boston investment banking firm in New York or pursue this award-winning business plan. Given the lure of investment banking and the pressing need to earn some income, I chose to spend the summer on Wall Street. I was not ready to leap into a new startup. I did not feel our business school venture had the right team, level of commitment, and sustainable business concept to be successful. However, the decision process I went through proved to be a valuable exercise, and positioned me for consideration of future startup opportunities.

The Wall Street experience was fun and stimulating. I learned about the capital markets and worked on a merger/acquisition deal involving an innovative hospital information systems vendor. However, I concluded that even though the financial rewards were there, I was not enamored with the business of financial transactions or the frenetic lifestyle that it entailed.

By the end of the second year of my MBA program, I had offers to work for an investment bank involved in health care finance or to work for Techmedica, a venture capital-backed, six year old medical device company. My exposure to entrepreneurs at UCLA excited me about the prospects of being involved in a startup business. At a "Brown Bag" lunch during my first year in business school, I met one of the founders of Techmedica and became fascinated with their business of using CAD/CAM and the latest in computer tomography (CT) imaging technology to make custom-fitted orthopedic devices, including hip and knee implants. I followed up to learn that they were also looking to expand their management team, with someone strong in finance and strategic planning.

I accepted Techmedica's offer, which represented 60% of my other salary offer. Yet with stock options, I felt the upside potential and experience in a startup environment were more what I wanted. And on a personal basis, I was in a position to take some risk; I was single, and my debt was limited to minimal student loans.

Startup Experience

Techmedica was located far from the dens of Wall Street in the light industrial, agriculture-based, bedroom community of Camarillo, California. The environment was casual, and the culture was set by a colorful founder, who was trained as a lawyer, yet spent the first decade of his career, working for an orthopedic device maker. The founder had the support of a savvy and wise venture capitalist, who raised the necessary funding to launch the company. The other key founders were an eccentric, artisan engineer and a systems developer, who had also earned his MBA at UCLA at night. The manufacturing operation was onsite, and so the employee base was a mix of blue-collar machinists and young, idealistic engineers.

By the time I arrived, Techmedica was a mature, profitable, six-year-old startup with a revenue base of $3 million. One of my first assignments was to plan and implement the sale of the company to a multinational company, based in Switzerland. The transaction created an "earn-out," which sufficiently incented me and the management team to stay on and grow the company. In addition, the parent company allowed Techmedica to maintain its operational autonomy. My focus was on building the company, recruiting key people, and leading the business development and financial planning efforts. Over the next six years, depending on the company's needs, I held a variety of "blocking and tackling" director roles in finance, marketing, and operations. During my tenure, the company grew to $15 million in sales and the workforce tripled in size to 140 employees.

By 1992, the demand for a premium-priced orthopedic hip and knee implant maker changed. With market pressures to reduce medical device costs, the notion that "one size fits all, particularly if it was cheaper" was replacing physician and patient preference for custom-fitted devices. Hospitals and insurance companies wanted clear evidence of the added clinical value of the company's devices, which required investment in long-term, clinical studies. Techmedica's founder thought that this market shift to managed care was temporary. He was slow to adapt the company's product line to the new market reality. This ultimately led to a management change. I stayed with the company another year, based on the optimism that the business would turnaround under a new president. In addition, I felt a commitment to the people I had hired. At the same time, I began researching other career opportunities.

Transition to Starting My Own Company

While health care reform was on the national agenda, the market for health care services was changing rapidly. I focused my job search on service companies that possessed a technology or systems component. In this process, I discussed opportunities with a range of companies from an established, publicly traded health care management company to a rapidly growing, sub-acute rehabilitation company formed by an ex-Booz Allen colleague. I also assessed my own risk profile, which had changed. I was recently married to a UCLA MBA, we shared two mortgages, yet had the security of her income and benefits. We were also getting settled into a new community in Southern California and we were expecting our first child.

After a lot of market analysis and soul searching, I concluded that my best career opportunity was to start a managed care software consulting firm. I was convinced of the need for software services that catered to the information needs of IPAs and physician groups. I had six months of savings in the bank, and a supportive, working wife. Rather than wait for another opportune time, I thought it was better to exercise my entrepreneurial option to have my own company. The blocking and tackling skills I had acquired at Techmedica, as well as my numerous health care industry contacts provided me the confidence to go forward with this venture.

I started my consulting practice with some basic premises:
* Empower the physician with the information to make cost-effective, evidenced-based decisions in a managed care environment.
* Understand the changing rules of the payor and model information systems around the clinical data needed for managed care.
* Capitalize on the latest technology, while mindful of its practicality in a provider's offices
* Be service-oriented.
* Create a values-driven culture, based on integrity and trust.

I worked closely with vendors and health care clients to develop, market, and implement information systems that combine financial and clinical data necessary for managed care and clinical decision support. My customers included a major biotechnology company involved in oncology, a hospital-based IPA, and several physician specialist networks.

The Turn in the Road to My Current Position

Some say if you survive three years in your own business, then you can consider yourself a success. After three years on my own, I had a financially rewarding, highly autonomous, yet still somewhat risky one-person consulting firm. I was not content to be just a consultant in health care information systems. I wanted to leverage my talents with a team of individuals who shared my vision and values.

In June 1996, I met Rick Lee, the founder and CEO of Accountable Oncology Associates (AOA). Lee's year-old company had some key components that I felt were necessary for a successful startup:

* Expanding team of respected clinicians and experienced managers
* Relationships and prior experience that were finance-able and led to initial venture funding
* Compelling disease management service concept
* Focus on large and unmanaged segment: cancer care

I was intrigued. However, this opportunity involved giving up my own firm, as well as relocating to Northern Virginia. My personal risk profile had changed as well. With two children and a third on the way, my wife was no longer working. Between us, we did not have to juggle two incompatible careers, but we were now dependent on my income.

As an interim step to find out more about AOA, I engaged in a part-time consulting position with the company. It was a chance for me to confirm the startup's prospects and work with the management team. After three months of due diligence, my wife and I concluded that this opportunity met both our personal and professional goals. In several ways, it meshed with the personal goals I had in starting my own company:

- Be part of an exciting startup at the ground floor
- Build a company based on values and vision that I shared

- Benefit from the intrinsic rewards of just doing something new as well as the economic rewards of successfully implementing the vision.

AOA is involved in the new health care service niche of disease management. First popularized by the pharmaceutical companies to market their drugs in a managed care world, disease management is developing into a business strategy of HMOs and risk-bearers, including large medical groups. With proven success in asthma and diabetes, these groups are focusing on the higher cost, more complex diseases such as cardiovascular conditions and cancer.

Over $50 billion was spent on cancer in the U.S. last year, and this figure is growing due to the increasing incidence rate and the introduction of higher cost treatments. There is wide variation in practice patterns and multiple specialists involved, leading to poorly coordinated, redundant or duplicative care. Cancer patients and their families are demanding more consistent information about the disease and treatment options, in order to make informed decisions. All of these factors have created a need for a more systematic, patient-centered, evidenced based approach to managing this disease.

For me, this career opportunity capitalizes on much of the experience I have gained during the last 17 years. From studying Jack Wennberg's practice pattern variation data, to working on the strategies of insurance companies, followed by my involvement in managed care information systems, I now hope to apply the skills and insight I have gained and have a positive impact on those involved in cancer care.

Predicting the Future

In reflecting on my career, I have found luck, perseverance, and a conscientious focus all contributed to the opportunities that I have enjoyed. I have also found the following to be helpful:

* Stick to my values and vision for successful companies
* Plan the work and work the plan
* Think outside the box; be open to new opportunities
* Always be sensitive to the "people" issues

I expect these principles to guide me in my current position and other health care service management opportunities in the future.

MEDICAL DIRECTOR: RESOURCES AND OUTCOMES

Gail Grant, MD, MPH, MBA

My Journey Into Management

My journey into medical management began while I was practicing medicine at a small community clinic in an underserved area of Los Angeles. There, witnessing the continual pursuit for adequate funding and the struggle of maintaining day-to-day operations with little management expertise, I became interested in the business side of medicine.

Reasoning that, unlike traditional medical practice with its one-on-one interactions, I could manage a similar clinic or other health care organization that could impact the health of larger numbers of people with the addition of some management training and additional funding. With that management expertise, I could even improve the efficiency of care. Those two goals appealed to me and provided the impetus for me to explore the field of medical management further. Thus, in 1987 I began my study of the US health care system.

Through my readings on medical management, I learned that, at that time (the late 1980s), many sources—such as the American Academy of Medical Directors and publications such as Health Affairs and Hospitals—were predicting a growing demand for physicians in management calling them by a relatively new term "physician executives".

Demands for increased efficiency, cost-containment, and high quality care, along with the perceived surplus of physicians and increased legal accountability of health care organizations, were all cited as factors in the growing demand for and entry of physicians into the management of health care organizations. There was a perceived need for physicians to become involved in the decision and policy-making aspects of health care. In addition, a need for enhanced collaboration between health care administrators and physicians was foreseen.

I was intrigued and ventured further by joining the American Academy of Medical Directors (renamed in 1988 as the American College of Physician Executives) and decided to test the water by taking a course in health care administration at a local university. That course was my first introduction to general management principles and the organization of the US health care system. As a result, my intrigue turned into fascination and I decided that I must learn more.

What? More School?! —The Case for Advanced Degrees

But learn more how? Formally or informally? Do I need another degree or would certificate or university extension courses suffice? After medical school, I swore I would never go to school again! But here I was, my fascination with health care delivery systems and management growing; apparent time to study available; and several programs in health care administration in my vicinity. I decided to give school a try.

My investigation commenced with a survey of courses, certificates and degrees available locally. I found many evening courses through off-site schools such as the University of Phoenix and at local campuses such as California State University at Long Beach. But I was unsure of what I actually needed, given that my vision of what my future position would be or the kind of health care facility in which I would be employed was still vague.

My investigation revealed that, in the past, on-the-job training was the only thing available to physicians, and it was also considered sufficient. With intensifying cost-containment and accountability pressures on the industry, however, emphasis was increasing on the attainment of specific management skills for physicians. At the time I was conducting my research (1987-88), the numbers of management educational programs was expanding through such institutions as University of Wisconsin, Madison and organizations such as the American Academy of Medical Directors.

Noting these trends and concerns, and given that I had the time, finances, and motivation to return to school I decided to enter the School of Public Health at the University of California, Los Angeles (UCLA). It was more a combination of opportune timing and situation, than any knowledge of a definite or future requirement for formal management training, which propelled me back to school.

Anyway, even as a medical student, I had always wanted a Master's degree in Public Health. Now I could do it, and I only had to devote one year to get it. At that time, those with previous doctoral degrees could earn a MPH with only one year of study. One year in school didn't seem that bad to me; I knew I had enough motivation to do that.

But, much to my surprise, while I was halfway through the program, I found that not only did I enjoy classes again, but that my thirst for more management training grew. Subsequently I applied and was admitted to

The Anderson School of Management at UCLA and began working on a Master's in business administration. That meant an additional two years of graduate school, which turned out to be two of the most intellectually stimulating and enjoyable years of my educational life! It was in business school that I learned the terminology, tools, and perspective of business.

It was also in B-school that I became exposed to one of the most important skills of business: teamwork. The ability to work as part of a team has turned out to be a tremendously helpful skill and a major catalyst in my career in medical management. With the repeated, required participation in teamwork, those behavioral characteristics that I had read about being common in physicians–independence, autonomy, one-on-one interpersonal interactions, and self-governance–became re-wired. I learned the value (and hurdles) of teamwork and could envision health care delivery as the multidisciplinary team of experts that it is supposed to be.

A Bonafide Manager: My First Position

As graduation approached, I had to decide on my next step. First I felt I had to confront the difficult task of whether or not to continue to practice medicine. Sure, I had heard and read all the reasons to continue doing it: maintaining credibility; to stay abreast with changes in medical technology; and to remain attuned to the day-to-day reality and logistics of seeing patients.

On the other hand, there were several reasons not to continue practicing medicine: the inordinate time demands of both, making it hard to do either (practice versus manage) well; the potential misperception by non-medical administrators of the physician executive as an adversary, one whose primary objective is to protect the interests of physicians.

I saw all of these as valid concerns, but, given my growing enthusiasm for management and my desire to put my newly learned skills to use, I decided to look for a full-time position with the initial goal of becoming a medical director of a health plan. Through networking, I learned that experience in utilization management provides a firm foundation upon which to build a career in medical management.

My first full-time management position was working as an Associate Medical Director at a national utilization management and network management firm. While there I learned the full spectrum of utilization management and case management. After one year I was promoted to Medical Director, and was responsible for supervising the other physicians in that office; assuring the quality of their medical reviews, leading the appeals process, helping to write and implement protocols, and performing reviews of complicated cases, such as bone marrow transplants and the assessment of new technology. I was call upon to perform limited data analyses for clients, another area in which I had interest and training.

I thoroughly enjoyed myself during that time. I found it easy to stay abreast of changes in medical technology and therapy since the process of utilization management required that I do so. In addition, by being exposed to a vastly larger number of cases than I would have been if I had remained in practice, I was able to review several rare and unusual conditions that I probably would not have even seen during practice. (when is the last time you saw of case acute porphyria!?).

Moreover, in the course of reviewing transplants and other complex cases, I was intellectually stimulated by the interaction with expert specialists from around the country with whom I frequently consulted. Faxed copies of recent medical literature and detailed case discussions by telephone were common and added to my job satisfaction. I found that I enjoyed the challenge of making and justifying difficult decisions that might affect a patient's medical care. It was like practicing medicine, but at another level.

And it also taught me an invaluable lesson: Choose your battles carefully. If you cannot provide sufficient, if not overwhelming, evidence to support your decision, or are unwilling to present that evidence convincingly to another physician or health plan representative, then you must reconsider whether there is a justifiable conflict to be resolved.

Being my first corporate position, this experience was also my first exposure to corporate politics. Certainly I had been exposed to politics in my previous work experience, but I found the politics of medical practice similar, but also decidedly different from those of corporate life. The difference lies in the degree of intensity and the priorities of those in various positions.

However, in corporate life, functioning among managers, I discovered a higher level of intensity for similar types of struggles—ego gratification, power struggles, and favoritism–but with decidedly higher stakes. Once again, that invaluable lesson came into play: choose your battles carefully. Fortunately, in my position as Medical Director for utilization management, few political battles faced me. After all, being the lead physician in that office placed me in a unique and valued position. Still, I was able to observe the political actions of others, which helped prepare me for future corporate challenges.

Critical Path: Charting a Career Course or "What do I do Next?"

Despite all the benefits and enjoyment I experienced as Medical Director, however, with three years of experience, I had reached the plateau of my learning curve, the routine day-to-day process of utilization review became rote and I desired new challenges. In addition, although I learned a lot, I was disappointed not really having put to practice all of the management tools and skills that I had acquired during my study of public health and business administration.

Moreover, given the lack of advancement available in my then-current organization, and the trend of declining clients and revenues occurring within the utilization review industry, I began to search elsewhere.

There must be another way to work with physicians, instead of being perceived as being against them, as frequently occurred during the course of utilization management. I needed something more proactive and collaborative in nature, instead of the reactive, adversarial atmosphere I had worked in for the past 3 years.

During this, my first management job change, I had time to re-assess my career direction. I was not being threatened by the potential of a lay-off, despite recent downsizing at my office, and my boss seemed pleased with my work. Hence, I had time to reconsider.

What I learned during that time of re-assessment is that attention to your own priorities is what is most important in making any type of decision, whether it be regarding a particular position or location. Of course, the first step is to establish priorities, including all aspects of your life, not just career considerations; deciding what is important to you can serve as a valuable guide during seemingly difficult or confusing processes.

Hence, I decided to limit my search to southern California. Over the next several months, I interviewed for several positions, mainly Medical Director positions for local health plans and other utilization management companies. Either nothing panned out or the positions were not appealing. I was almost discouraged when a position developing disease management products became available.

The position was part of a new disease management unit formed as a result of a joint venture between an applied health services research company and a pharmaceutical company. It seemed like an ideal, cutting-edge opportunity: an opportunity to be creative through product development (in which I was extremely interested); to work with a team (which I enjoyed); and the chance to participate in a proactive approach to utilization management, working with physicians.

In contrast to traditional utilization management, disease management held forth the prospect of building more collegial and positive relationships with physicians and patients. And, finally, perhaps I could at last put some of that training in public health and health services, if not management, to use!

My first charge was to develop a broad-based disease management program for respiratory conditions by leading a multidisciplinary team of physicians, pharmacists, and research assistants. The program would provide a complete set of tools and outcomes measures for use by patients, physicians, and nurses, all with the objective of promoting cost-effective care. These tools would promote what had been identified by the medical literature and experts as the best currently available care, or "best practices" of care.

Interestingly enough, those tools were mainly in the form of software. Hence, in addition to working in product development, and on a more proactive method of utilization management, I was able to indulge in my long-standing interest in informatics. Here I received my first exposure to software design and development. It seemed like an ideal combination, an ideal position.

Those exciting times came to an abrupt end when that company was suddenly, and surprisingly, acquired by a large multi-hospital company, Columbia/HCA. Hence, I made my exit before the first round of lay-offs and was lucky enough to land a position in resource and outcomes management at a large, academic medical center.

Thus, I am able to continue working with physicians and other health care providers to bring them tools and information which allows them to deliver high quality, efficient care. This new position has also brought me closer to the providers of health care, with whom I now work directly instead of purely telephonically (as in utilization management) or indirectly (as a vendor performing product development).

And, with the ever-increasing need for data and information by the providers and managers of health care, I am still able to indulge my interest in informatics, but this time I am more extensively involved in data analysis, while continuing work in identification and development of best practices and outcomes measurement.

Lessons Learned:
Critical Skills or Survival of the Fittest

*   Networking—Keep that ear to the ground!

I find nothing of more value than my colleagues. Initially I viewed networking as a means to learn what others are doing and what problems they are confronting in my positions or areas similar and dissimilar to mine. Perhaps due to my visual myopia, I have an aversion to conceptual myopia, so networking was my way of getting a different perspective on and ideas about my work and career, a way of thinking "outside of the box".

Later, however, I learned that having a network of colleagues had an added advantage: as a valuable resource during a job search and as a safety net for job security, particularly in these tumultuous times of frequent mergers and acquisitions in the health care industry. During my most recent job search, I put that network to work extensively and it paid off. Even if colleagues can't point you in the direction of an opening, they can recommend you to others who do have an opening. And those types of recommendations go a long way!

*   Know your industry, not just your company or position

In addition to networking, I found that constant surveillance of the industry is another necessity for career development and management. Trying to avoid myopia once again, I read industry publications that provide a broad coverage of all segments of the health care industry in all parts of the country, with particular focus on my local geographic area.

As time permits, I read about other industries that interest me as well. By reading about interesting developments in other totally dissimilar industries, you may be able to spot trends or innovations that may be applicable to, or affect, our industry.

The advantages of keeping abreast of the health care industry include being able to anticipate market changes, trends, and opportunities that may help either your career or your company. Perhaps you could identify or even create that position or company you've always desired!

Besides, with the health care industry being multi-faceted and such an integral and personal part of everyone's life, I find the reading entertaining at the very least and perpetually fascinating at best.

* Self-development–Learn, learn, learn!

Along with industry surveillance, continual self-development is key. Given the turbulent times now current in the health care industry, I've found it prudent to constantly supplement, update, and improve my skills. Similar to the continuing medical education necessary for the provision of good medical care, continuing education in your management area of expertise should be considered a requirement for successful career management.

In addition, I focus on learning new skills as much as possible. Not only does this added knowledge and ability make me a more desirable candidate for another organization or position, but it also keeps me in a constant learning mode that primes my mental faculties for new challenges and perpetuates flexibility. And in these days of industry transformation, I feel that those two qualities–flexibility and the ability to meet challenges—will become requisites for survival in this industry.

The Future

I am still pursuing placing my management training and skills into actual practice. Ideally, I would like to combine my expertise in resource, disease, and outcomes management with my interest in informatics and my general management training. Perhaps towards that endeavor, my future journey will take me perhaps to senior management of a health care delivery system or other type of health care enterprise or maybe to my own business.

With its usual uncertainty, the future is certain to bring with it a host of new challenges, opportunities, and learning experiences. These are exciting times and health care is an exciting industry in which to work! I eagerly anticipate the continuation of an equally exciting journey, one that is stimulating, gratifying, and successful.

Management Search Firm CEO

Deborah Shlian, MD, MBA

I never thought about any career other than medicine. My plan to become a doctor was articulated around the age of five or six–likely the result of being the first born child of a doctor. My father was always the role model I emulated and although he neither encouraged nor discouraged my interest in medicine, his life as a "healer" was for me the only path I wanted to follow. Still, growing up in the late 1950's and early 1960's, a time when family and career roles were still fairly rigidly differentiated by gender, this view required considerable adjustments from parents, friends, and particularly school counselors who regarded nursing or teaching as much more acceptable roles for women than physician. Indeed, the idea of a career itself was simply "something to fall back on," to be dusted off should a husband die or family economics suddenly suffer. Full-time wife and mother was the generally accepted appropriate role for a woman of that era. However, never one to be stopped by convention, I remained single-minded. Interestingly enough, my determination changed the thinking of those around me, so that within time they accepted my decision without argument. By the end of high school even my guidance counselor was resigned to my becoming a doctor.

It wasn't until the end of medical school when I had to make a decision about specialty that I again faced considerable opposition to my career choice. In 1972, although there had been some brief mention of Family Practice as a new specialty, there were very few residencies in the country and even less guidance as to where to find them–particularly on the East Coast. So, despite my fascination with the concept of a "new, complete physician," I chose the road of least resistance and matched with a Hopkins radiology training program. It was a chance vacation to Los Angeles during my internship year that changed the course of my clinical career. My husband (we married in my junior year of medical school) arranged for a meeting with the head of Family Medicine at Kaiser Permanente. Our preventive medicine curriculum in medical school had included a comprehensive study of what was considered by many traditionalists to be a renegade operation (or worse, socialized medicine) i.e. a group model Health Maintenance Organization. The notion of salaried doctors working in a prepaid multi specialty group that functioned as a partnership was different, if not heretical in the 1970's, when the vast majority of doctors were in solo private practice. But my husband and I had found the concept more than intellectually interesting. It seemed to make a lot of sense and we were anxious to see the system up close.

Dr. Irv Rasgon was my first real role model and mentor. Chief of Family Medicine at the Sunset facility, he charmed us from the moment we met him. Irv was the quintessential Marcus Welby–he even looked the part. A great clinician, outstanding teacher and natural leader, he was passionate about Family Practice and Kaiser. "Why specialize and become so narrowly focused when you can be a Family Practitioner and take care of the whole patient?" he asked us. Irv took us on hospital rounds and his patients, from the very young to the very old, obviously adored him. Moreover, it was clear that his peers in other specialties respected him. When he offered us the opportunity to come to Los Angeles, finish our training as FPs and become Kaiser staff physicians, we readily accepted. I left radiology; my husband left ophthalmology; together we headed out to Southern California where we completed our training, took and passed Family Practice boards and joined the Southern California Permanente Medical Group as partners.

Lest one think that this was an easy decision, I should point out that the opposition I encountered to my leaving a specialty like radiology for this "new fangled non-specialty" as many regarded Family Practice was quite formidable. My dad, who is an internist, was particularly unhappy. He regarded the decision as the mistake of a lifetime. His generation had venerated specialists, viewing doctors with broad, general knowledge and skill as somehow less doctors than mere dabblers. Many friends and colleagues felt I was giving up the guaranteed security of a high paying field for a "pig in the poke." Needless to say, I did not agree. I believed then and still do to this day (despite the renewed opposition to Family Medicine) that the most effective (cost and quality) healthcare delivery system has a well trained, primary physician at its core, managing the ongoing care of patients, referring to "narrow" specialists such as cardiologists or endocrinologists in very few, but appropriate situations.

The decision to leave radiology and come to Kaiser was pivotal. Looking back, the ten years I spent as a clinician in the Kaiser group provided the kind of education in medicine and management that no didactic program in either medical or business school could ever provide. We were at the forefront of what has been nothing short of a revolution in healthcare–working in a fully integrated system that allowed us to deliver quality care (as much of the full spectrum of pediatric and adult medicine that was feasible in an urban hospital/clinic setting) without the stress of wondering whether our patients could pay for the care they required (what we know today as managed care). We had the advantage of being hospital based, making our inpatients easily accessible during the day while we saw our scheduled outpatients in our offices which were located in the same building. Similarly, we could often grab "sidewalk" consults from specialists who worked down the hall or just upstairs–thus avoiding long appointment delays for our patients. Lab, X-ray and other ancillary services were a floor below–another efficiency. We were given a half day a week of paid education time which my husband and I used to teach residents of UCLA. Medical students from both UCLA and USC spent one month electives at our Kaiser offices and I was even able to satisfy my clinical research interests with such projects as a study of "Screening and Immunization of Rubella Susceptible Women" which was published in JAMA. My department held regular quality assurance and peer review sessions; we developed clinical guidelines long before it was fashionable. From a quality standpoint, I believed then and still do today, that the group model is an ideal way to practice medicine. Unfortunately, it is also extremely capital intensive and in the kind of highly competitive market that characterized California even in the 1980's, some of the original idealism began giving way to market pressures. As a primary care clinician, I became increasingly frustrated at my inability to influence policy. I felt that front line physicians had the best perspective for identifying and correcting problems within the system. Yet despite the fact that legally the group was a partnership, in reality it was governed no differently than most corporate entities: top down and the top physician was a surgeon who often stated that patients did not care about having their own physician, that they were primarily motivated by easy access to the system and that any clinician–doctor, NP, PA, would do just fine. It didn't matter. Needless to say, this undercut the fundamental principles of Family Medicine–taking care of the whole patient and being able to provide continuity of care by the same physician. In fact, this chief refused to accept the validity of our early studies (later, a group out of Vermont published the same findings) showing that patients with their own primary care doctor had fewer emergent visits and less inappropriate hospital admissions–both a significant cost savings and quality improvement. Again with hindsight, I now realize that his intransigence on this and other healthcare policy related issues created the opportunity for me to make yet another critical career decision. My husband and I both decided to leave Kaiser.

With no one to provide career guidance, we began investigating how we could use our skills and understanding of healthcare to have a greater impact on the system. I wrote several articles as well as a consumer health guide for a national health maintenance organization and we both spoke at various venues around the country about problems involved with the delivery of care in the managed care environment. During the first few months of my "retirement," we were persuaded to start part time law school at Whittier School of Law in Los Angeles with the intention of developing an expertise in health policy and health law. However, not long after starting my first semester, I was recruited to a management position at the UCLA Student Health Service (SHS).

I became Director of the Primary Care unit of SHS which serves all thirty-three thousand undergraduate and graduate students on the university campus. As many as four hundred patients per day were being seen in our clinic–most of whom used SHS as their only source of medical care. What attracted me to the position was the opportunity to take many of the lessons learned from the Kaiser system and adapt them to this setting. In particular, I wanted to change the orientation of Primary Care from essentially a triage area to a comprehensive ambulatory care facility staffed by clinicians competent enough to have admitting privileges at UCLA Medical Center. That meant firing non-board certified physicians and hiring only well-credentialed family practitioners, pediatricians and internists–a process fraught with legal/risk management/personnel issues that I had to quickly research and understand. In addition, I wanted to integrate our service with the outstanding teaching programs available in the medical school. That required honing a new level of diplomatic skills, delicately balancing the egos and agendas of various department within the school. But happily, within a relatively short time we had developed an impressive educational and research program that helped to attract medical students and graduate students as well as superior clinical staff. Our quality of care, patient and personnel satisfaction all measurably improved.

As my administrative duties expanded, two significant issues surfaced which ultimately led to yet another critical decision affecting my career path. First, was the question of whether I could be a successful manager and maintain a clinical practice without compromising both. Increasingly, I felt caught between what I perceived as two equally important and demanding responsibilities. In the past, there seemed to be consensus that despite the difficulties, one could not be an effective and credible leader of clinicians without concurrently having an active clinical practice. In fact, with the exception of a very few full-time regional medical directors, that is still the model Kaiser uses today for most of its physician administrators. On the other hand, in many other healthcare organizations, the role of physician executive has expanded so that those who wish to assume broad management responsibilities within these companies realize they must relinquish the clinical role, instead bringing the strong patient care background as a resource to a new, more comprehensive job description. Still, I must admit, for me it was not an easy decision, though looking back, it was one that has made all the difference in my success as a manager. As an executive who was also a physician, I was in the unique position of developing and enhancing collaboration and integration of the medical and administrative staffs in the daily management and operations of the organization.

The other issue had to do specifically with my expanding operational responsibilities. Up to that point, everything I had accomplished as a manager was achieved without the benefit of a formal educational foundation. For example, I was asked to develop a budget, but had never taken a finance or accounting course. I was asked to make staffing projections but had never learned the kind of operations research tools needed to create a truly robust model. Without a working knowledge of the language and concepts of business, one becomes totally reliant on non-medical administrative personnel whose orientation to the bottom line may at least sometimes run counter to quality. This revelation convinced me to switch from law school to business school and in 1988 I completed an executive MBA program at UCLA's Anderson School of Management.

Two things occurred as a result of the MBA program. First, my job description expanded to include policy formulation, strategic planning, broader budgeting responsibilities, contracting for outside specialty care, risk management, and helping to develop and implement a computerized patient record to capture data for outcomes measurement. I became part of the senior management team, attending meetings heretofore open only to the non-physician administrators.

Second, I began receiving telephone calls and letters from recruiters alerting me to other opportunities in medical management. Suddenly, I was advised that my experiences as both a clinician and manager in two managed care settings, coupled with my MBA degree, made me a strong potential candidate for many organizations looking to import that kind of expertise. Both flattered and curious, I decided to explore a few of these possibilities.

I had never worked with recruiters before and so had no idea what to expect. Someone would call my office, identify themselves as representing a particular job opportunity, then inquire as to whether I wanted to be considered as a candidate and if not, did I know someone else who might. Surprisingly, the recruiter often had minimal information about the organization, asked few relevant questions about my management experience and none about my interests and career goals. Moreover, when I did interview I often found the opportunity quite different from that described to me–from the nature of the job to the organization itself. It seemed clear that these recruiters were not serving their clients optimally: sending inappropriate or disinterested candidates is a waste of time and money. However, as I've come to learn, even negative situations can become potential opportunities.

As a result of these disappointing searches, I suddenly realized that an unfilled niche existed: full-service, comprehensive search consulting in the managed care market. True, there were plenty of people out there calling themselves recruiters. But no other firm dealing in that specific market had someone with my credentials. As a respected physician manager continually interfacing with the national medical community, I felt I could bring a unique perspective to searches. My credibility could further enhance a client company's reputation as I discussed available opportunities with prospective professional candidates. The other value-added component would be my willingness to develop long-term relationships with fellow physicians, guiding them through the search process—even putting some on the management career path initially, then mentoring them along the way. As I had personally experienced, no one in the search industry seemed interested in investing the kind of time (and thus capital) it takes to develop an individual executive's career, nor does anyone (as far as I know) have the kind of hands-on understanding of the talent pool to give appropriate advice.

Despite the sense that I could do it better, it took many months of soul searching before I actually made the decision, eventually transitioning from physician manager to medical management search consultant. My position at UCLA was tenured, I had spent six years developing staff and programs I believed in, I loved working with the students and I had been told by my professors in the management school that more new businesses fail than succeed—especially consulting firms. According to an article in Fortune magazine, only one new consultancy in five will thrive. If I really wanted to be an entrepreneur, I had to be willing to take that risk.

Armed with a business plan including mission statement, I finally decided to take the plunge. Beginning in 1990, I slowly built a firm that initially concentrated only on physician executive searches. As a career counselor to potential candidates, I often spent untold hours evaluating career goals, life priorities, reworking resumes, developing better interview techniques and assisting with contract negotiations. The best payback has been the satisfaction of having launched many successful management careers, watching these individuals make significant contributions to a variety of healthcare organizations, including other healthcare consulting firms. I help these organizations build high performance management teams by identifying appropriate entry, middle and senior level non-physician as well as physician management personnel vital for their success. That means fully understanding the organization, from governance to culture; evaluating specific personnel needs; conducting local and national salary surveys as the market changes; keeping close tabs on the interview process from start to finish including contract negotiations and following up regularly with both the client company and new employee for at least a year after placement is made to be sure an optimal transition has been achieved.

In 1994, my husband Joel joined me as president of the company. In 1996 we incorporated as Shlian & Associates, Inc., moving our main base of operations to Florida while maintaining our West Coast office. Both Joel and I are active in professional healthcare organizations such as the American College of Physician Executives and the American Association of Health Plans, always keeping abreast of changes in medicine and in particular, managed care. We also regularly contribute articles and chapters for various textbooks on current management issues. Additionally, we have developed affiliations with over a dozen associates with offices across the country, all with strong healthcare backgrounds, who we call upon to assist with specific searches. In this way, we are able to service our clients effectively while still maintaining the boutique nature of the company. Many small business owners feel compelled to expand in order to demonstrate success. However, according to Douglas Handler, an economist at Dun & Bradstreet, longevity rather than growth is the real measure of achievement. "Companies that last three years will usually make it," he claims. "indeed, if you begin a company to capitalize on the wisdom and personal service of a key individual–namely you–big is bad. Adding staff and projects can spread the core value of your firm so thinly that customers are dissatisfied." David Birch, founder of Cognetics, an economic analysis company noted for its studies of small firms says: "In the knowledge-based service firm, there are no economies of scale."

After over nine successful years, this seems to make sense. We continue to enjoy repeat business from clients who hire S&A knowing we are much more involved in the details, we personally know prospective candidates and we can do the job more efficiently and less expensively than larger firms with high rise offices and huge overhead. While a large firm may be able to coast on its reputation, Joel and I never can. If we perform poorly for clients, our business fails. Bottom line: being your own boss is definitely not for the faint of heart, but if your vision triumphs, the success is yours alone and therefore all the sweeter. For me, the shift from a management position in a highly bureaucratic and hierarchical organization to CEO of my own company has been the most exciting and positive experience of my professional life.

As a final point, I am constantly asked about the value of an MBA, particularly to physicians contemplating switching from clinical medicine to management. I can say with great confidence that for me, the MBA education and the degree itself have made all the difference in my career. As a manager, I was able to directly apply the classroom knowledge to my work, enabling me to expand my role to include much more of the business/operations side of the organization. As a search consultant, I regularly work directly with CEO's, CFO's and COO's who appreciate the fact that I can speak their language. Often intimidated by physicians, they feel comfortable talking to a "fellow MBA." As the CEO of my own business, the training in accounting, finance and marketing has been particularly useful.

Notwithstanding the value of a management education for me, I would advise any physician considering going back to school that an MBA will not provide the same kind of ticket that the MD did. By that I mean, having the business degree on your resume, even from one of the elite schools, is not sufficient to land you a job as a manager, nor is it still generally required for most positions. What really counts and is still generally required for most positions: management experience and the ability to show that you have produced tangible results for an organization. This is often identified by such measures as greater market share, larger profits, decreased costs, reduced utilization, better outcomes and increased patient satisfaction.

An MBA should never be viewed as the means to "get out of medical practice." In fact, I would submit that if you really hate clinical medicine, medical management is not for you. It can be every bit as demanding and frustrating as clinical practice. Moreover, as the rate of change sweeping America's healthcare delivery system has accelerated, healthcare companies are reinventing themselves, developing competitive strategies that mean greater risk and more uncertainty than ever. Medical managers entering this brave new world, particularly those at the middle level, need to understand the landscape and be prepared to deal with it. Rather than one by default, the decision to be a manager should be a positive career choice. As the traditional separation of administrative and clinical matters is becoming obsolete, the modern physician manager must be a manager first and a clinician second. Bringing a clinical background to the new role of manager can certainly enrich the job, but does not substitute for specific management skills and training. Whether medical management as such will ever become a recognized specialty is less important than the fact that only those who understand both the language of business and of medicine will be able to straddle the various camps that now control the practice of medicine in this country.

For me, the career path from clinician to medical manager to CEO of a management search firm has been anything but a straight one. With each opportunity, came a choice and a certain risk. But in the end, it has been those forks in the road that have made all the difference.

PHYSICIAN EXECUTIVE IN TRAINING

Dave Snell, MD, MBA

I had not, until recently, envisioned myself being in any sort of management role in medicine. I can remember being asked at a medical school interview whether or not I was interested in using my political science college major to serve as a physician in legislative affairs. It was the furthest thing from my mind. Instead, I followed the trends of the time and expressed my desire to become a Family Practitioner. I went through the clinical training process, ending up in an Internal Medicine residency, as an emergency room/Internal Medicine clinical attending at Harbor/UCLA Medical Center and finally in an Anesthesiology residency and private practice. Eventually, I became more and more aware of the fundamental lack of "process" in my education as a physician. This bothered some innate sense of order and I found myself constantly trying to make things work; organizing new pager systems, rewriting call schedules to allow for days off and sleep, trying to understand financial contracts, and so on.

All of this led to being elected to the management board of my thirty-person anesthesiology group and running the anesthesia department of a smaller hospital that we had contracted with. The mantra of the day (the early 1990s) was that one needed to become involved in Utilization Review and hospital Quality Assurance committees in order to become a "management type". I did so, but had a real sense of frustration when I saw how little action followed review of cases that obviously needed remedial work. I felt very much constrained by being labeled as an anesthesiologist, not expected to be much more than a technician, and certainly not capable of managing medical affairs. I also saw the difficulty that physicians had in dealing with managed care and wondered if I could be a part of a new wave of physicians that could take responsibility for the health care system and turn it into a process that was much more user (physician and patient) friendly. I had absolutely no idea of how difficult that would prove to be.

After two years of managing an anesthesiology group and failing to make much progress in mergers, acquisitions or common sense, I began to think about business school. Management experts suggested that besides providing the necessary skills to rise in the hierarchy, a business degree was a signaling device for physicians that wanted to commit to management. At this point in time (1993) I was not aware of any healthcare specific MBA curricula, so I applied to several traditional Executive MBA programs. I chose UCLA for a number of reasons. First was the structure of attending classes every other weekend and second, was its reputation. In retrospect, I made an excellent choice, since I was one of four physicians in a class of seventy-five business professionals, the majority of whom were company executives on the fast track. Having an opportunity to interact with non-healthcare people provided a far richer learning experience than I might have had if I had chosen a program solely geared to health care professionals.

Sadly, there was not much support from the university for career progression. Nor did the degree immediately place me in the ranks of highly employable medical managers. The problem was my lack of significant hands-on experience. The first mistake (out of many in this management trail) was to assume that a graduate degree would substitute for experience. It does not and I have interviewed a number of physicians that have expressed the thought that they are ready for senior management roles after finishing a healthcare MBA.

I found myself going to numerous interviews for Associate Medical Director positions (and any other job that I thought might give me the valid 'experience'), but always facing the same Catch-22: no experience, no position. Fortunately for me, fate intervened. I had been working with a physician healthcare consultant who also did recruiting for physician executive positions. She had adopted the informal role of mentoring me to this next stage and advised of an opportunity to interview for a regional medical director position in Tennessee. Initially, the location was a definite no-go, but I found out that the Chief Medical Officer for the plan (BlueCare—the Medicaid HMO plan for Blue Cross) was a friend from medical school. It also was a chance to jump start my career, since I wouldn't have to transition through the Associate Medical Director position stages that primarily involved utilization review.

I started working with Blue Cross in May, 1997, with a new MBA and a small amount of medical management experience. I was constantly amazed at the level of sophistication that the CMO had in contracting, medical management strategies, and the ability to determine how the process should go. I, on the other had, could play well with others and follow directions, so after an initial orientation period, was sent to the corporate office in Nashville to work with the big boys. While I was outgunned by the expertise shown by the people at Columbia, I did have the experience of working in a managed care environment (in California) which was more than many physicians had in Tennessee. I found that my willingness to admit that the system was difficult to navigate and then do something about it for physicians and medical groups, led to the building of relationships. I learned a phenomenal amount in a short time about disease management, population health theories, contracting, physician manipulation of coding, etc., etc. I think I was able to do a fairly credible job and build a good team of case managers, project managers and UR people just by using my background in medicine and surgery, but above all, caring for my staff and helping them perform.

After a year in Nashville, I had the opportunity to become the medical director for a medical device company back in California, but elected to take a promotion to the position of Medical Director for Clinical Services and Operations for BlueCare, a position located at headquarters that was a sort of first among equals of regional medical directors. I initially viewed this as a stepping stone to a CMO position. However, the nature of corporate politics, the difficulty of convincing my wife to move to the South (I had been commuting between Nashville and California), and a number of personnel issues beyond my control, led me to seek another position outside the company.

After looking at several options, I elected to become a healthcare consultant with Milliman & Robertson in Seattle. My selection by M&R for the post was due to a number of factors; my personality and ability to work with non-healthcare teams, the MBA (signaling device), and my managed care experience (the 16 months at Blue Cross). My own reasons for joining M&R were, in hindsight, not sufficiently well thought out. While I had utilized M&R's guidelines during my time at Blue Cross, I was unaware of the firm's primary purpose, that of providing actuarial and healthcare consulting services. I was also totally unprepared for the change in environment. At Blue Cross, physicians had a major role in the process; at M&R, the firm relied on physicians as consultants, but the vast majority of partners in the firm were actuaries and this was reflected in the culture and day-to-day operations. I had difficulty adjusting to the change and don't feel that I ever understood the participants, the process or the product.

I worked in two different areas during my tenure at M&R. First, I did basic healthcare consulting in conjunction with the actuaries, clinicians and IT teams that were in our practice. I was able to contribute to several projects such as medical management overviews, review and projection for ICU use for a suburban hospital, appropriateness of use of Medicaid funds, etc. Consulting was a challenge and a learning experience because you never knew where the project was going to take you. I became very good at finding answers (which is what a consultant should be doing), and also producing a clear, written analysis with options for the client. For a period of time I was traveling extensively, and, while exciting initially, the familiar airport/airline delays, the nights in strange hotels, and the time away from family took their toll. The consulting itself was sometimes difficult to find rewarding because of the all too common situation where the client might put the report on a shelf and/or ignore your recommendations completely. This was in spite of the large amount of work (and sometimes heart and soul) that you put into a project. In retrospect, it takes a certain type of individual to excel at, and enjoy a consulting career, and I wasn't that type.

I was also involved in the guidelines practice (part of another M&R division), where I ended up researching, writing and reviewing guidelines in the written and online formats. M&R's guidelines had been referred to as "credenza ware" because of the tendency for the large printed volumes to remain on the shelf once purchased. Part of what I was involved in was to work with the IT group on projects that would transition the guidelines to an electronic format. In retrospect, this was the most satisfying work I did at M&R, not only because it resulted in a concrete product, but also because of the people involved in the projects.

The weather in Seattle proved to be another negative for me and my family. We lived through the worst winter there in 50 years—daily rain for 91 consecutive days from the time I arrived! So, when it was announced that the guideline division was being separated from the rest of M&R, I felt it was time to make a change. The company had experienced a slowdown in their healthcare consulting and I felt that not only would this continue, but that there were far more aggressive business seeking consultants than me in the marketplace. Additionally, my expertise and skill set was in operations, in being able to get a diverse group of people motivated toward a common goal in healthcare, and derive some satisfaction from that. When an opportunity came to return to southern California as Regional Medical Director for an IPA management company, I took it to avoid having to live through another winter in Seattle (and face the WTO protesters in front of M&R's downtown office).

Currently, I am the medical director for the northern Los Angeles region for an IPA management company that has grown significantly in little over a year. The basic model of the company is to buy financially-strapped IPAs (and which aren't these days?), institute firm medical management techniques with the buy-in and help of local physicians, and sell 50% of the IPA back to the physicians at cost. Critical to this process is the prompt use of appropriate data on physician referrals, procedures and cost. Again, I had the feeling of being over my head, but the learning curve for me, thanks to my time at Blue Cross and M&R has been significantly shorter. I still find myself doing those things in medical management that I didn't care much for, such as calling uncooperative physicians and doing reviews and appeals, but obviously, these are necessary evils of the job. Anyone who wishes to be in medical management will need to find their particular skill set and comfort level in dealing with this. Hopefully, I will convince the IPA physicians that making our recommended changes will improve the quality of care delivered to their patients at the same time allowing for a profit for the IPA, the company and these same physicians.

I have found in the three years that I have been involved in medical management that it is certainly not what I thought it would be. It has been a tremendous challenge to deal with physicians who are intentionally abusing the system and your trust. On the other hand, it has been rewarding to work with motivated doctors and receive their gratitude for making good things happen for both them and their patients. Lessons learned along the way include:

* Experience still counts substantially in this field; given the choice between someone with an MBA in healthcare and one who has been 'walking the walk' for two years, the experience will always win out. You can send your managers to MBA programs; you don't want your MD/MBAs to learn at the expense of the company (and your reputation)

* Practicing physicians in the managed care arena will continue to frustrate you at any level; compounding this is the necessity of establishing relationships and some form of trust in those relationships. This is not always pleasant, but necessary. If you don't have this skill set, don't think about medical management.

* It is difficult to function as a Medical Director (and enforce the rules, procedures and terminations) in a group in which you have had a previous clinical relationship. Unless you have excellent powers of persuasion, becoming the Medical Director of your own IPA can lead to straining of relationships that you thought were forged in steel.

* Medical management is a complex field, with its own rewards and penalties. It is definitely not the solution for a physician who is simply bored or frustrated with clinical practice. Even with all the negatives of clinical practice today, it still offers substantial financial reward, independence and control relative to the role of a managed care medical director. Nevertheless, for those innovative professionals with a medical degree who wish to try other options (healthcare.coms, healthcare analysis for an

investment bank, venture capital firm associate), there are tremendous opportunities.

* Determine what your particular skill set is and maximize your ability to perform. Use networking, recruiters and/or search consultants, mentors, friends and even family to consider available opportunities. To obtain the 'best fit' position, you might have to move to another part of the country or commute (which is exceedingly stressful).

For me, I think the ideal position in medical management would be to head a group of physicians who had agreed in writing and committed themselves to pursue the business of medicine in a particular way, and wanted the CMO/CEO to help lead them to that understanding. Until I receive that offer, I'll continue to chip away at the large amount of work that accumulates on a daily basis and buy lottery tickets

WHERE WE HAVE COME FROM AND WHERE WE ARE HEADED

Mark Strom, MD, MBA

I think I would have been a better doctor if I had had an MBA and been a CEO first. Why? An MBA is designed to provide the tools to achieve goals, create objectives, measure results and make an impact. It helps one to learn how to make decisions in a less than perfect world in conditions of uncertainty. It helps to define how value can be measured, how risk can be assessed and how damage can be controlled or mollified. These are all things that were never taught in medical school.

Unlike the corporate focused MBA curriculum, medical school training prepared us for a cottage industry environment. We were encouraged to be the final and autonomous authority for patient care and to regard our profession as being so important that everything else was secondary: hobbies, personal interest and social intercourse, not to mention marriages.

While our basic value as physicians is to "first do no harm", we have ignored that adage in today's managed care environment. Too often we have let the insurance industry dictate the medical services our patients can have, the amount of time they can stay in a hospital and even the prescriptions we can order for them. Because we are not well organized as a profession, we just do what we have always done, only under stricter and more invasive rules. Like ostriches, we have simply put our head in the sand and pretended the storms will go away. But, the changes won't go away. We cannot and should not keep doing the same things we have always done. We can keep our heads in the sand, or we can respond to the buffeting changes that every other industry in this country has faced and responded to.

As physicians we were not given tools to use to measure the quality of our care, adapt to a changing environment, or even consider change. We were taught and we believe that we are somehow exempt from the changes buffeting every other industry because we are physicians and can do what no one else can: care for ailing patients.

Healthcare in Context

The fact of the matter is we tolerate more errors in the care of our patients (e.g. medication errors, surgical complications, even deaths) than we do in the production of our airplanes and automobiles.

We live in a system that has evolved so many rules that patients actually die while they are waiting for care decisions to be approved.

I can clearly remember the poor 40-year-old man who died the day before I was authorized to operate on him. He had done everything right according to our new rules. The system did everything wrong. He had gone to his Primary Care Doctor and waited for the referral to a cardiology specialist. Then we waited for the cardiologist's surgical referral to me to be authorized. Before I could operate, he died. And, we let this, or something close to this, happen every day. Wait for this authorization or that referral, when lives are at stake. Try to explain to his wife and their two toddler children that our system of patient care is working and that we put the patient first.

We have let this chaotic system dictate the terms of patient care to us and we have not challenged it. As physicians we cannot get the information we need on our patients in a timely manner. We don't even know when or how much we will be paid. And still, we have done nothing.

Because our medical training is so focused on our personal clinical skills, we were not taught how to manage our medical business or our patient's care in an evolving and rapidly changing environment. We may want to return to the 1960's and 1970's when we could make independent decisions and be accountable to virtually no one, but that is like wishing to have hair again when we are genetically destined to be bald. And even if we could go back, doing what we have always been doing is clearly not the best answer.

From Cottage Industry to Medical Mastery

Fewer than 10% of all physician offices have browser technology in the workplace. We resist the Internet because we fear the lack of privacy or we don't know whom to trust. So, rather than defining how we can make technology and the Internet work for us, we bury our heads again. We may lament that our patients come in with lists of drugs or treatment options they have found online, but instead of finding ways to work with this new technology, we complain about it. Instead of looking at is as a tool or a partner to make our lives better, we curse it because it is making our lives miserable in deciphering where our patients have gotten the information and how reliable that information is. We say information on the Internet is not secure and rail against the potential lack of privacy, yet we give our credit cards to virtual strangers and machines everyday, and litter our offices with paper patient files that are left here and there for anyone to see from the receptionist to patients in the waiting room.

The truth of the matter is, we physicians don't always know if we are making the best clinical decisions. Another truth is that we don't even know how to make good financial decisions. We rush into contracts with managed care organizations and assume the financial risk in doing so, but we don't have the financial and cost information to know whether we are doing well or not. Would a CEO join into blindfolded arrangements like that? Not on your life.

We have blindly assumed that because we know how to diagnose and treat patients, we know how to care for them in a managed care setting or that we know the long-term impact of our patient care decisions. And that is where an MBA and Internet technologies can make a difference.

By having good information, we can analyze the impact of our clinical decisions. If we have that information now, we can make sure our patients do not have to wait for what literally can be a matter of life and death. By accumulating information we can create data that can help us analyze our clinical decisions. Best of all, if we have the financial data simultaneously, we are no longer managing in the dark, but can take control of our clinical and financial needs. And, we can move out of our cottages into the 21st century.

Setting Goals, Values and Objectives and truly Managing Care

As a surgeon, I like to be in control and to take control. I started my medical career in Cardiac and Thoracic Surgery at the Garfield Medical Center and UCLA. Wanting to make an impact on patient care in more than the operating room, I moved into administration to help assure the quality of clinical services and create clinical standards for our surgeons and our surgeons in training. As a physician reviewer and consultant and a peer reviewer for the Board of Medical Examiners in Iowa, I have evaluated professional physician services. I have designed strategic marketing plans, negotiated contracts and written and managed quality assurance and utilization review procedures for biotech companies, pharmaceutical companies, and other healthcare services.

What has struck me in all of this is how little common, reliable information is available to the practicing physician when he or she needs it the most: when the patient is with them. I am also struck by how little feedback most physicians have about their practice and referral patterns. I am constantly struck that when confronted with change, most physicians–like most humans—resist learning from new technologies or new ways of doing things.

Finally, as a consultant to venture capital firms, I am stunned with what most practicing physicians are willing to risk when contracting with or creating their own managed care organizations. The expectations they have of the data they need are vastly different than the data required by most venture capital firms. As physicians we were not taught how to create goals and measure objectives. We were taught to diagnose and treat. We were not taught how to evaluate our effectiveness or even to question our effectiveness.

As physicians, we have focused so much on our clinical capabilities, whether it is diagnosis, treatment, or surgery, that we have not asked ourselves what we could be doing better for our patients and for ourselves that would improve the care of our patients. This is why I think I would have been a better physician if I had had an MBA and been a CEO first. I would have asked different questions, demanded different information. I would have questioned more of the things we did, how we did them, why we did them and if what we were doing made a difference to the quality of care our patients received.

And now, as we step into the 21st Century we have the opportunity to do just that. Set goals for patient care, which is the only reason why most of us should be in this business anyway. If we are going to accept risk for the care of patients, then we need to set the terms and conditions of that risk—both clinically and financially. If we are to provide better care for our patients, we need to document what is working for and against them in our current "system" and then accumulate and use that data to support our case. If we are to eliminate the medical errors and mistakes we made, we need to aggregate that data and find out what is going on, where and why it is happening and make the changes we need to make to assure those errors and mistakes don't happen any more.

We can do all that. But, we have to change how we are doing things. We have to leave old ways behind. In truth, we all know they are no longer working. If we face that we have much better ways to do things, then change is no longer a frightening prospect with yet another thing to learn. With new tools we can have that data. This means, for the first time, we have a chance to shape our future and the future of clinical care and finally fulfill the oath to serve we all took as physicians.

Unpredictable Paths—
Not for the Faint Hearted

Susan Acevedo, MD, MBA

I decided to pursue a career in medicine to make an impact, but little did I know I would be taking such a non-traditional path. I started on this non-traditional path at age twelve, when I decided I wanted to be a physician. This may not sound that non-traditional, except for the fact that I articulated this desire while growing up in a predominantly Hispanic, working class neighborhood. While most of my classmates were focused on graduating from high school, I was focused on getting into Stanford University as a pre-med student.

The Role of Health Care Provider

After several exams, dollars and years, I had a bachelor's degree in Human Biology and a Doctorate in Medicine from Stanford University. During those years, I became increasingly aware of the need for physicians in the Hispanic community, but realized there was an acute need for bilingual, primary care physicians. As a medical student in an academic, research oriented institution it was not easy sticking to my guns and continuing my pursuit to be a primary care physician. I wanted the opportunity to use my old skills (speaking Spanish) and my newly acquired, clinical skills in an environment where I could make an impact. Again, it was time to continue on my non-traditional path, so I went on and continued my training at Los Angeles County-University of Southern California Medical Center.

My year at "County" was like no other year in my life. The stories are true. You treat some of the most ill patients, see the most amazing cases, and meet some of the most dedicated individuals. I used all my old and new skills, and learned a few basic survival skills (e.g., how to start an I.V. despite multiple scars from needle tracks, drink really bad vending machine coffee, make friends with the nurses taking care of your patients, etc.). At this point, I still wanted to be a practicing physician, but I was getting restless in training and wanted the chance to hurry up and make an impact. I wanted to get out in the "real" world and take care of inpatients and outpatients in the Hispanic community. I knew I could always come back and finish my residency. I accepted a position in a small, clinic in Santa Ana, California.

After internship, I easily adapted to three 12-hour shifts per week at the clinic. What was a bit more challenging was, on occasion, not speaking a word of English during those 12-hour shifts. I became quite fluent in Spanish, and learned how to manage very complex cases on a shoestring budget. Again, I learned more basic survival skills (e.g., how to make friends with drug reps who can supply your indigent patients with free medications, how to integrate Western and alternative medicine beliefs). I moved to a small, private practice down the street after 18 months—the hours were better and I had an opportunity to be considered for a partnership. During the next 18 months, I become more intrigued by managed care concepts and decided to join a staff model HMO after the practice disbanded and the partners went their separate ways.

Initially, the staff model HMO was a haven for getting away from the rigors of understanding billing and reimbursement nuances. The folks at "corporate" handled the "business" side of medicine while I was busy handling the "clinical" side of medicine. That suited me fine. I had a healthy sized panel of Spanish speaking patients, and had more resources and services available to my patients and me. Nonetheless, I still found myself playing the role of physician/nurse/therapist/dietician/social worker because of my Spanish speaking abilities and the lack of Spanish speaking ancillary staff and bilingual patient education materials. After a year, I began to actively participate in quality improvement committees, both at the local and corporate level. I also began to pay more attention to the memos from "corporate", and attempted to understand what they were trying to communicate to the clinicians. It was evident that "corporate" did not understand the clinician's reality and world, and the clinicians did not understand the "corporate" realities and world.

After only six years of practicing in a variety of primary care settings, I did not feel like I was making an impact. I was treating one patient at a time, but realized that to make a bigger impression I needed to be in a position where the decisions I made were going to affect more patients and the "system". I felt the need to understand how to handle not only the "clinical" side of medicine, but also the "business" side of medicine. I realized I could either gradually work my way up the physician leadership ranks of an organization, or take a faster approach to a physician leadership role by obtaining an advanced degree. Just ten years ago, this was not something you talked about openly, especially among other physicians. I quietly decided to "temporarily" leave the practice of medicine to pursue a Masters in Business Administration (MBA).

Exploring New Roles

I briefly considered attending a quick, one year Masters in Public Health (MPH) program, but instead opted for the two year MBA. The thought of a one-year sabbatical was initially more attractive than the two years away from a steady income. The need for a foundation in business basics (e.g., accounting, finance, economics) and the potential career opportunities with an MBA outweighed the benefits of a one-year MPH return on investment. I was not certain of the job opportunities with either degree, but wanted a program that was going to be academically rigorous and challenging. I was also interested in exploring opportunities in other industries outside of health care.

The Anderson School at the University of California at Los Angeles (UCLA) is a great school and was a wonderful learning experience. The program stressed team projects, which were refreshing since my pre-med and medical school programs, emphasized solo efforts and no opportunity for creative brainstorming. I truly enjoyed learning about different companies and different industries. I found case studies on companies with complex business problems fascinating, but more importantly relevant to applying lessons learned to the healthcare industry. My classmates learned about the health care industry from me (the only physician in a class of over 350 students), and I learned about their backgrounds and previous work experiences. I once again learned new survival skills (e.g., how to use a Mac and PC in 8 hours during Orientation Week, how to find the right teammates to survive challenging courses).

At first I considered exploring career opportunities outside of health care–investment banking, brand management, etc. The reason for this change of heart was based on the fact that I had experienced burnout in medicine. However, after a few months away from seeing patients and complying with formularies, I missed many of my patients and confirmed that my heart and soul was still in the medical field. During the second quarter of my first year, I visited the career center to see what was available to MD/MBA candidates. The career counselor took one look at my resume, and informed me that I had such a unique set of skills as a physician that the center did not have any positions for anyone with my background. She basically let me know that I was on my own for finding a job and new career.

I initially attended different workshops and receptions sponsored by various recruiters. Though companies that refine oil or make disposable diapers actively recruit MBAs, I did not see my future in projecting gasoline sales or marketing consumer goods. I attended events sponsored by any and all companies providing healthcare products or services. The pharmaceutical/biotech companies appeared the most promising, until I told them I was a physician and they quickly suggested research opportunities in their laboratories. I passed on the opportunity to wear a white lab coat again, since I reminded myself that I was looking for a new way to change the system and make an impact. One day I attended a presentation by management consultants, and heard about health care consultants that assisted clients on quality improvement and process improvement engagements. Getting paid for helping hospitals and physicians improve clinical quality and enhance operations. It sounded like an exciting, non-traditional path for me.

I quickly learned the value of networking and marketing since not very many employers were actually looking for an MD/MBA. Not only were they not looking for an MD/MBA, but also they were less interested in one that was not board certified. I was fortunate to connect with a fellow MD/MBA who had her own physician executive search firm, and who happened to be working with a management consulting firm. Though my resume didn't fit with the specs for a medical consultant (i.e., board certification), she spoke with the company and talked to them about how she felt I had a unique background that might fit in with their organization. I subsequently scheduled an informational interview with the Director of Human Resources. After the interview, she did not know if the Health Care Consulting practice was hiring but she went ahead and sent my resume to one of the partners. Two key partners in the healthcare consulting practice interviewed me. I suggested they invest in me (teach me how to be a consultant), while I in turn would contribute my clinical expertise and exercise my newly acquired management skills in helping build the practice. They were interested in me, and I was interested in working with them. I joined the firm.

The Role of Consultant

I spent over four years in health care consulting at Ernst & Young. I used my first hand knowledge of managed care in California to prepare physicians and hospitals in other parts of the country for managed care. I conducted and managed a variety of utilization management projects. This allowed me to use my clinical training while talking to physician leaders, and my business training while talking to hospital administrators. I saw all stages of managed care, from coast to coast. I saw the "walking wounded" in California (with the most aggressive lengths of stay in the country) to providers in small communities that had utilization patterns that were consistent with their fee for service reimbursement. My credentials either helped establish credibility and trust among both hospital administrators and physician leaders, or made each side more distrustful of me since they each knew I could easily see right through their group's excuses and arguments.

After being promoted to Senior Manager, I had more opportunities to develop many of the skills that I still rely on today. I became more proficient at writing proposals (many for multi-million dollar projects), making presentations to hospital and payer executives, and creating work plans for increasingly larger and more complex projects. I also had the opportunity to manage projects of increasing complexity and risk. But those in the Information Technology group soon were realizing the best opportunities. I began to notice that more physician groups, integrated delivery systems and managed care organizations were looking at technology solutions to solve their operational problems. Again, I saw the need to acquire additional credibility and therefore new skills and experience in the area of information technology.

The Role of Information Expert

To make the transition from operations to information technology, I had to rely on my contacts and network. I had come through with recommending a friend to a friend, and continued to nurture the relationship. My friend joined my other friend, and I kept in close touch. I expressed my interest in making a switch from consulting to software. Again, I emphasized how my clinical skills and consulting experience would be useful in implementing their products. Through several months of discussion and waiting for the right time, the time was right and an offer was extended. It is true that many job leads and opportunities come through friends and acquaintances–it is whom you know and not necessarily what you know.

I decided to go from a Big Five management consulting firm that represented "Corporate America", to a software start-up company in Berkeley, California. I joined KnowMed Systems, now known as "iKnowMed", two years ago. I started at ground zero–learning the software business. I initially supported and managed software installations, but always continued to develop my client relationship building skills. I quickly learned the difference between a server and a router, and am still learning the difference between HTML and XML. I went on to develop and manage the education and training programs for the company, including programs focused on training physicians and nurses to use our interactive, electronic medical record. The application can integrate clinical guidelines, and present diagnostic and/or treatment options at the point of care. It currently supports medical oncologists in ordering and managing complex chemotherapeutic order sets or "regimen management". It also supports physician documentation and E&M code selection, but more importantly alerts clinicians of potential drug-drug and drug-condition medication errors.

More recently, I have taken on the role of Associate Medical Director at iKnowMed. In this capacity, I am currently an active member of the Sales/Business Development Team, which is responsible for expanding the number of customers and users. I will also be responsible for bringing key community and academic oncologists together to form an active partnership between physicians, pharmaceutical/biotechnology companies, and patients. The goal of the network is to exchange clinical data and share clinical knowledge.

Nine years ago I decided to stop treating patients, and start treating the system. I have had a great time going down this non-traditional path, and do not regret my decision(s). I wish more physicians would join me. Just remember, this path is not for the faint hearted and be prepared for a wild ride.

A Lifelong Relationship

Eleanor Brewer, Med, MBA

The health care field is alive, exciting, exploding, regenerating, reincarnating, in other words: it's on fire. And like the fires of nature which bring forth new growth and a renewal to the earth, health care is in the process of renewal. With this renewal comes traumatic change, realignment, and refocus. Some describe it as a process of transitions, transactions and transformations. Whatever it is, it's not easy. But, it is exciting and if one is willing to change, opportunities abound.

One way to take advantage of the opportunities and challenges of a field in such turmoil is to be able to analyze the relevant drivers of the change, learn from other industries who have or are experiencing similar changes and innovate amid the turmoil. The Anderson School at UCLA is an ideal place to prepare oneself and receive support for one's efforts in such a dynamic environment.

The Anderson School is known for its innovation, its entrepreneurship, its professors who continuously push the boundaries of knowledge, its insights into how businesses change and realign, and its progressive use of technology. The Anderson School at UCLA brings together many publics in the microcosm of administration, faculty, classmates, alumni and business leaders.

Like the Anderson School, the health care industry now has the active involvement of virtually every thread of the fabric of our society—patients, families, employers, governments, stockholders, as well as health care professionals and non-professionals. As a result, roles are expanding and colliding. Health care is no longer an industry isolated from the economic tensions of the global world in which we live. The health care industry is metamorphosing from a collection of community-focused, medium-sized, fragmented providers of care to major businesses with stockholders who need to be factored into its complicated business equations. Many are prophesying the ultimate vision of health care. A vision which must include a significant demographic shift, the aging of the baby boomers, which will put enormous pressures on health care financing.

There is much to be done before the dawn of this new vision. How will health care providers regain the trust of their patients and patient families? How will the ethical issues involving such difficult questions as financing, end of live, access to care and the uninsured be debated and resolved? What are the structures for this industry which must balance the needs of people and finite resources? Will the economic forces of the business complete a redistribution of wealth in the field? Will quality be a measured commodity which actually drives health care purchasing decisions? Will the field be able to respond to an assertive consumer society?

The Anderson School in collaboration with other UCLA schools provides a forum for these health care debates. It sponsors a research center on health issues. And, it supports a large and active Health Care Alumni Association. These efforts in health care are combined with many services available to Anderson Alumni.

Each year hundreds of alumni participate in continuing education activities sponsored by Anderson. These take place all over the world throughout the year. Notices can be found in the highly acclaimed newspaper Anderson Assets along with updates on faculty, students, administration and alumni. Each edition provides an in-depth look at a topic of current interest and details the perspectives of The Anderson School family members who are leaders in the area. The Anderson School has an endless supply of professionals to call upon for insights into virtually every area of world economics. As a result, it is a wealth of information and ideas for everyone associated with the school, especially health care professionals.

The Internet also serves to keep Anderson family members together. Alumni can subscribe to e-mail lists where events are planned, advice is exchanged, personal news is shared and insights abound. And with the Lifelong e-mail Forwarding Address system, no matter how many times a person's e-mail address changes, classmates can always reach him or her through a permanent Anderson address.

The Parker MBA Career Management Center offers links to dozens of career resources on the Internet as well as The Anderson Bulletin and The Search Bulletin which have hundreds of job listings for experienced MBAs in all areas of the country. Graduates within the past 10 years can conduct a confidential job search online using MBA Central. Graduates can list position openings at the Career Center and participate in on-site interviewing of qualified candidates.

The Rosenfeld Library offers full access to its world class collections to all members of the Anderson faculty, students and alumni. It provides a wealth of information for health care professions ranging from mergers and acquisitions to predicting the impact of organizational change.

In short, a lifelong relationship which continually enriches one begins with admission to the school. A Master of Business Administration degree from the Anderson School at UCLA in combination with a health care professional degree positions one to participate as a leader and a shaper of the health care industry of tomorrow.

Final Words

Deborah Shlian, MD, MBA

The question so often asked by individuals aspiring to healthcare management positions is "how can I enter the field and how can I move up the ladder?" As the reader can see from the personal experiences described here, there is no single route leading to career success. However there are definitely some ways to increase your chances. We've put together some helpful tips from the contributors.

Strive for Excellence

Look for ways to polish your skills and use those skills as building blocks to move ahead. The healthcare manager today must have an understanding of the details of the business of healthcare including finance, accounting, strategic planning, information systems, organizational behavior, human resources and relevant legal issues. Even if you have a formal degree you will need to integrate your reading and study with experience. So take every opportunity to obtain practical experience within the organization. The medical world is full of committees, task forces, et cetera that can offer an exposure to administration, working with people and systems and problem solving.

Educate Yourself About Your Organization

To borrow a medical analogy, organizations, like organisms, are organic and as such have specific structure and function. The structure of a medical organization would cover such issues as the type of legal entity, mode of governance, financing and so on. On the other hand, the overall way a specific organization functions is affected by what is often called its "cultural climate." For example, how do professional and non-professional staff interact? What is the extend of bureaucracy and hierarchy? How much operational responsibility is given to physician versus non-physician managers? Understanding these aspects of your organization is critical to moving ahead.

Network

Get to know people both within and outside the organization whom you can tap for information and support. This is a skill men seem to develop early in life–perhaps as a result of their involvement in team activities as children. Whatever the reason, women need this ability too.

Take the Initiative

Don't expect handouts. In the corporate world, upper management promotes people who find and seize opportunities. Actively seek projects to take on. If you see something that needs changing, develop a plan and present it to senior management. Whenever possible, take on projects that give you visibility within the organization.

Be a Risk Taker

Be willing to grab opportunities where and when you find them. Whenever you read profiles of people who have had high level management positions in and out of medicine, you find that they generally got where they are by taking on new assignments. For both men and women today, having supportive significant others and families is critical. Creativity helps too. For example if you want to participate on a committee and accommodate family needs, suggest doing some of the work through conference calls and e-mail.

Learn to Negotiate

Refining your negotiating skills and learning to achieve win-win solutions will maximize your leverage as a manager. Several of the books listed in the Related Reading section discuss negotiation strategies.

Select the Right Subordinates

If you're in middle management, the personnel you select will determine how well suited you are for a senior position, since senior managers are generally judged not by how well they do, but by how well their staff does. Senior managers must have a clear vision of the future of their organization. They need to be leaders for change.

Find a Mentor

This is not always easy, but can make all the difference in moving up.

ABOUT THE EDITORS

Deborah Shlian, MD, MBA

Deborah Shlian, MD, MBA is a board certified Family Practitioner and MBA with sixteen years of clinical and management experience (ten years as a partner with the Southern California Permanente Medical Group in Los Angeles, followed by six years as Director of Primary Care, UCLA Student Health Service). Nine years ago, she formed her own consulting and executive search firm which has proven to be enormously successful. The firm's focus has been to act as consultants to health care clients, helping them build high-performance management teams vital for success in this competitive environment. Deborah is active in health care management organizations such as the American College of Physician Executives (ACPE) and the American Association of Health Plans (AAHP)—always keeping abreast of the changes in medicine. From 1978 until her move to Florida, she taught clinical medicine as well as managed care principles to Family Medicine residents at UCLA. Additionally, as president of the UCLA Anderson Health Care Management Alumni Association until 1997, she created a Health Care Management Group, a forum for prominent health care leaders in the greater Los Angeles area that continues to meet on a regular basis at the management school to discuss current issues within the health care industry. Finally, Deborah has authored many articles and several books related to health care management and careers in the industry including two chapters in a1997 text published by McGraw Hill entitled *Critical Concepts in Medical Practice Management* and a chapter in a text entitled *In Search of Physician Leadership* jointly published by the American College of

Physician Executives and Health Administration Press in 1998. In 1997 she was selected to be section editor for the "Changing Roles of the Physician" section in *New Medicine*, a quarterly review journal which serves as a forum for emerging ideas, applications and innovations influencing the new healthcare marketplace.

Clint Patterson, PhD, MBA

Clint Patterson, PhD, MBA currently manages a 20 bed physical medicine and acute rehabilitation unit as well as ancillary therapy services for the hospital and two affiliated programs that are part of a leading integrated delivery system in southern Los Angeles. Originally trained as a clinical psychologist at the University of Miami, Dr. Patterson developed an understanding of the clinical side of healthcare delivery. As a provider with experience in HMOs, publicly-funded, as well as for-profit entities, Dr. Patterson has been involved in the effective delivery of care and management across a wide array of programs. In 1996 Dr. Patterson graduated from the Anderson School where he focussed on operations and information systems in the full time MBA program. After completing his studies, Dr. Patterson worked as a consultant for a leading healthcare management consulting firm before returning to a direct role in management on the provider side of the healthcare delivery system. Dr. Patterson is an active member of the Board of Directors of the Beach Cities Health District. He was elected in 1998 and he has been effective in assisting the organization develop an evidence based approach to investing in public health efforts. During the first half of his four year term, Dr. Patterson has also assisted with the adoption of a formal approach to program evaluation and prioritization of community needs.

ADDITIONAL RESOURCES

Related Reading:

Time to Heal: American Medical Education from the Turn of the Century to the Era of Managed Care. By Kenneth M. Ludmerer. Oxford University Press. 1999

Disease Management: A Systems Approach to Improving Patient Outcomes. Warrant E. Todd and David Nash, editors. American Hospital Association, 1997.

Essentials of Managed Health Care, edited by Peter Kongsvedt. Aspen Publishers, 1997.

Market Driven Health Care: Who Wins, Who Loses in this Transformation of America's Larges Service Industry. Regina E. Herzlinger. Addison-Wesley, 1997.

Complete Q&A Job Interview Book. Jeffrey Allen. John Wiley & Sons, 1997.

The Role of Pharmacoeconomics in Outcomes Management. Nelda E. Johnson and David Nash, editors. American Hospital Association, June 1996.

Critical Concepts in Medical Practice Management, edited by Bob Tallon, MD, MBA. McGraw Hill Healthcare, 1996.

Health Against Wealth: HMOs and the Breakdown of Medical Trust. George Anders. Houghton-Mifflin, 1996.

Adams Job Interview Almanac. Adams Publishing, 1996.

Getting Past No: Negotiating Your Way from Confrontation to Cooperation. William Ury. New York: Bantam Books, 1993.

The New Leaders: Guidelines on Leadership and Diversity in America. Ann M. Morrison. San Francisco: Jossey Bass Publishers, 1992.

Getting to Yes: Negotiating Agreement Without Giving In. Roger Fisher & William Ury with Bruce Patton, editors, 2nd edition. New York: Penguin Books, 1991.

Men and Women: Partners at Work. G.F. Simons & G.D. Weissman. Los Altos, CA: Crisp Publications, 1990.

You Just Don't Understand: Women and Men in Conversation. Deborah Tannen. William Morrow & Co. 1990.

That's Not What I Meant! How Conversational Style Makes or Breaks Your Relations with Others. Deborah Tannen. New York: William Morrow & Co., 1986.

The Manager as Negotiator: Bargaining for Cooperation and Competitive Gain. David A. Lax and James K. Sebenius. New York: The Free Press, 1986.

You Can Negotiate Anything. Herb Cohen. New York: Bantam Books, 1982.

Internet Resources

The Internet and the World Wide Web are quickly emerging as useful communication links for job opportunities. If you have a modem, a computer and some easy to use web browser software such as Netscape Navigator or Internet Explorer, you can readily access the information. If you know the URL (Universal Resource Locator) or address of a particular Website or home page, take advantage of directories such as the New Riders Official World Wide Web Yellow Pages (http://www.mcp.com/nrp/wwwyp/). Or use search engines such as Google (http://google.com) or Yahoo (http://yahoo.com)), or Lycos (http://www.lycos.com/).

Job Related Websites:

Newspaper classified ads are still a resource for career opportunities, but more and more getting online is a way to plug into the job market.

- * The Monster Board (http://www.monster.com) has one of the Web's largest job databases, allowing you to search for openings according to your skills and interests. Or try finding a job at CareerBuilder (http://careerbuilder.com) which also offers advice on career advancement, relocating to another city and other employment issues.

- * Shlian & Associates, Inc (http://home.earthlink.net/~dshlian) is an example of a recruitment firm that lists active job opportunities for physician and non-physician healthcare executives. The

Website also supports a newsletter with interesting tidbits about the healthcare industry.

* If you want to spruce up a resume or cover letter, visit the Website called About Work: Work Resumes & Cover letter (http://www.aboutwork.com/jobs/res_cover/) for practical writing tips.

* If you want information to help with relocation such as relative cost of living in once city versus another, try these two Websites: http://www.homefair.com/homefair/cmr/salcalc.html and http://www.holland chamber.orghcccstlv.htm.

Made in the USA
Lexington, KY
20 December 2010